Technology and Regulation

For other title published in this series, go to
www.springer.com/series/7133

Zicklin School of Business Financial Markets Series

Robert A. Schwartz, Editor
Baruch College/CUNY
Zicklin School of Business
New York, NY, USA

Other Books in the Series:

Robert A. Schwartz · John Aidan Byrne
Antoinette Colaninno
Editors

Technology and Regulation

How Are They Driving Our Markets?

 Springer

Editors
Robert A. Schwartz
Zicklin School of Business
Baruch College, CUNY
One Bernard Baruch Way, B10-225
New York, NY 10010
robert_schwartz@baruch.cuny.edu

John Aidan Byrne
169 Chestnut Terrace
Rockaway, NJ
USA

Antoinette Colaninno
Zicklin School of Business
Baruch College, CUNY
One Bernard Baruch Way, B10-225
New York, NY 10010
antoinette_colaninno@baruch.cuny.edu

ISBN 978-1-4419-0479-9   e-ISBN 978-1-4419-0480-5
DOI 10.1007/978-1-4419-0480-5
Springer Dordrecht Heidelberg London New York

Library of Congress Control Number: 2009926068

Printed on acid-free paper

Springer is part of Springer Science+Business Media (www.springer.com)

Contents

Preface

This book is an augmented account of *Technology and Regulation: How Are They Driving Our Markets?*, a conference hosted by the Zicklin School of Business at Baruch College on May 1, 2007. The text includes the edited transcript of the full conference: four panels and the major presentations of three distinguished industry leaders – Ian Domowitz, Managing Director, ITG, Inc.; Erik Sirri, Director of the Division of Market Regulation, US Securities and Exchange Commission; and John Thain, who was CEO of NYSE Euronext at the time of the conference. The book also includes a related paper by Paul Davis, Mike Pagano, and myself: "Divergent Expectations," *Journal of Portfolio Management*, Fall 2007.

My co-editors and I have worked diligently to make this book, like all the other popular books in the series, more than an historical record. John Byrne, Antoinette Colaninno and I have edited the manuscript heavily for clarity and unity of ideas. New material is included from interviews after the conference with many of the speakers. Our intention has been to round out the panel discussions with more details, while being careful not to sacrifice the essential nature of the original dialogue. We worked closely with the panelists throughout the editing process to ensure that we did not put words in their mouths. Indeed, all of the panelists approved the final draft. We thank them for their assistance. We are also most grateful to our sponsors who made this conference possible (see page xi). Their funding and endorsement of our program are deeply appreciated.

Technology and Regulation was the tenth conference in our annual Zicklin School of Business Financial Markets Series. Each year our theme has been somewhat different from the last. But the fascinating thing is that many of the same underlying issues persist each year if you dig down deep enough. The debates simply do not end. I applaud this complex and dynamic industry for providing an interminable array of issues!

Our first panel, under the leadership of my colleague Professor Rich Holowczak, focused on technology while the second, under Nasdaq's Chief Economist, Frank Hatheway, turned to regulatory initiatives. In the third, moderator Joe Gawronski, COO of Rosenblatt Securities, called our attention to, "What the Buyside Needs." Joes's panelists were from the buyside and the sellside, which shows that it is not only the buyside that has opinions about what the buy-side needs. In the final panel, Nic Stuchfield, who at the time of the conference was Director of Corporate

Development at the London Stock Exchange, brought us to the big picture. We heard views from both sides of the Atlantic that included insightful perspectives from both the equity and derivative markets.

I started the day off by presenting some of my own thoughts about the theme of this conference. As we know, three forces drive our markets: technology, regulation and competition. Competition, however, is not an external (exogenous) force similar to technology and regulation. Competition is a product of technology and regulatory developments. Also, our 2006 conference, Competition in a Consolidating Environment, focused on competition. So, our 2007 event concentrated on the other two forces, technology and regulation.

Technology and regulation were examined as collective as well as separate matters throughout much of the conference. The interaction between them is of great interest as is clearly evident in the conference subtitle, "How Are They Driving our Markets?" For instance, lately, dark liquidity pools have grown tremendously, attracting much attention. What is the reason for this growth? Is it technology or regulation, or both? The answer, undoubtedly, is both, but just how is it all playing out? On another level, recent regulatory initiatives, such as the trade-through rule, could not be implemented without technology. Reciprocally, at least some of the technology innovations may not have been introduced without a regulatory push by Washington. Technology advances occur on several fronts. Firstly, there is the power, speed and capacity with which computers transmit and process information. Secondly, computers have the ability to tie together disparate information sets, different marketplaces for the same product (e.g., stock), and different products (e.g., stocks and options). Finally, computers have been used to change the very structure of a market. NASDAQ's introduction of its opening and closing crosses is an excellent example. The NYSE's Hybrid Market is another. One might also note the novel application of computer technology by two newer entrants, LiquidNet and Pipeline. And then there is the International Securities Exchange, an automated marketplace within which market makers play an integral role.

It pays to keep in mind, however, that technology is itself neutral. Whether its impacts are desirable or not depends on just how technology is being used. To be sure, computationally fast computers are great. But what are the market quality implications of lightening-fast order handling that gives importance to microseconds? And what about lightening-fast trading that has resulted in algos being used along with "on-the-spot" human decisions?

Regulation will continue to have a tremendous impact on our industry. Back in 1997, just one decade before the 2007 conference, the Order Handling Rules come on board. Today, in the US markets, we also have Reg NMS and the trade-through rule. The trade-through rule will have a major impact on the operations of our markets. In Europe, market structure regulation is also taking center stage in the form of MiFID, the Markets in Financial Instruments Directive. As we all know, each major regulatory initiative on market structure, starting with the Securities Acts Amendments of 1975, has generated substantial debate. I, along with many others, have been sympathetic to the regulatory goal of making our markets fairer and more efficient. But, based on my own view of the enormous complexity of the economic issues involved, I have taken a more free-market stance toward the evolution of market structure. Nevertheless, I will note one way in which the interaction between technology and regulation can be very beneficial. Life may simply be too cushy for a market center that faces only weak competition. A market center with monopoly powers may be too slow to adopt new technology that would increase market efficiency. Consequently, regulation can shakes things up. The Order Handling Rules are an excellent example. The trade-through regulation in Reg NMS is another.

Even the very threat of regulatory intervention can have positive consequences. Ernie Bloch and I pointed this out in a 1978 Journal of Portfolio Management paper that we co-authored.[1] At the time, the New York Stock Exchange had an order consolidation rule, NYSE Rule 390. In brief, the rule required NYSE member firms to bring customer orders in exchange-listed stocks to the exchange for execution. While the requirement was viewed by many as an unjustified monopolistic constraint on competition, others in the industry adamantly defended it. In light of this, Ernie and I wrote, "Because of the expressed fears of industry, the SEC has been able to use the threat of removing 390 as a club to get the industry to move itself in the direction of an NMS (National Market System)."

Following major regulatory interventions such as those which we have seen, new entrants can emerge and, as they do, the marketplace subsequently fragments. Then, as time passes, the pieces get put back together again. In the process, a market center may have re-engineered itself. Re-engineering has, in fact, occurred throughout Europe, starting with London's Big Bang in 1986. In the US, NASDAQ has reengineered itself, and the NYSE has now completed that mission too. The 1997 Order Handling Rules ushered in a period of intense competition in the US, followed by a period of re-consolidation. Why the re-consolidation? Because markets exhibit huge economies to scale, they convey enormous network externalities.

Let us hope that, after re-consolidation, some old problems will have been solved. But will the new regulations have "unintended consequences"? Will new problems appear? Will these lead to new calls for further market structure regulation that will be followed by further rounds of fragmentation, intense competition, and then re-consolidation once again? Three to five years hence, will our markets be more efficient than they are today? Will we see yet lower transaction costs and a level of intra-day volatility that is better contained? These are among the questions that were considered at Baruch on May 1, 2007. As one might expect, the debates were lively. We hope that the excitement is conveyed in this book.

Robert A. Schwartz

---

[1] Ernest Bloch and Robert A. Schwartz, 'The Great Debate over NYSE Rule 390,' *Journal of Portfolio Management*, Fall 1978, pp. 5–8.

Conference Sponsors

American Stock Exchange
EdgeTrade, Inc.
International Securities Exchange
Investment Technology Group, Inc.
JonesTrading Institutional Services LLC
Knight Capital Group, Inc.
Liquidnet, Inc.
NYSE Group, Inc.
Pipeline Trading Systems LLC
Security Traders Association
Security Traders Association of New York (STANY)
The NASDAQ Stock Market, Inc.
White Cap Trading LLC

List of Participants

Leonard Amoruso	Knight Capital Group, Inc.	Senior Managing Director and Chief Compliance and Regulatory Officer
James Angel	Georgetown University	Associate Professor of Finance
Douglas Atkin	Majestic Research	President and CEO
Leslie Boni	UNX, Inc.	Managing Director
Harold Bradley	Ewing Marion Kauffman Foundation	Chief Investment Officer
Kevin Callahan	JonesTrading Institutional Services LLC	Head of Sales and Strategy
Donald Calvin	National Stock Exchange	Board of Directors
Paul Davis	TIAA-CREF Investment Management LLC	Retired Senior Managing Director
Ian Domowitz	Investment Technology Group, Inc.	Managing Director
Alfred Eskandar	Liquidnet, Inc.	Director of Corporate Strategy
Fred Federspiel	Pipeline Trading Systems LLC	President
Bill Freund	Pace University	Professor
Robert Gauvain	Pioneer Investments	SVP and Director of US Trading
Joseph Gawronski	Rosenblatt Securities, Inc.	President
Daniel Gray	US Securities and Exchange Commission	Senior Special Counsel
William Harts*	Harts & Company	Management Consultant

*At the time of the conference, Mr. Harts was Managing Director at Banc of America Securities.

Frank Hatheway	The Nasdaq OMX Group	Chief Economist
Richard Holowczak	Zicklin School of Business, Baruch College, CUNY	Director, Wasserman Trading Floor – Subotnick Center
Richard Ketchum	NYSE Euronext	CEO, NYSE Regulation
David Krell*	International Securities Exchange	Founder

*At the time of the conference, Mr. Krell was President and CEO of the International Securities Exchange.

James Leman	Westwater Corp.	Principal, Head of Capital Markets
Robert McCooey	The Nasdaq OMX Group	SVP, Capital Markets Group

Oscar Onyema	American Stock Exchange	SVP and Chief Administrative Officer
Michael Pagano	Villanova University	Associate Professor of Finance
Bob Pisani	CNBC	Correspondent
Andreas Preuss	Deutsche Börse AG	Member of the Executive Board
Joe Rosen	RKA, Inc.	President
James Ross	NYSE Euronext	VP, NYSE Crossing
Stephen Sax	FBN Securities, Inc.	Vice President
Robert Schwartz	Zicklin School of Business, Baruch College, CUNY	Marvin M. Speiser Professor of Finance
Michael Scotti	Traders Magazine	Editorial Director
Daniel Shaffer	Shaffer Asset Management, LLC	President, CEO and Chief, Investment Officer
Douglas Shulman*	Internal Revenue	Chairman

*At the time of the conference, Mr. Shulman was Vice Chairman of NASD.

| Erik Sirri | US Securities and Exchange Commission | Director, Division of Market Regulation |
| Nic Stuchfield* | MTS S.p.A. | Board of Directors |

*At the time of the conference, Mr. Stuchfield was Director Corporate Development at the London Stock Exchange.

| Larry Tabb | The TABB Group | Founder and CEO |
| John Thain* | | |

*At the time of the conference, Mr. Thain was CEO of NYSE Euronext.

Grant Vingoe	Arnold & Porter LLP	Partner
Joseph Wald	EdgeTrade, Inc.	CEO
Robert Wood	University of Memphis	Distinguished Professor of Finance
Steven Wunsch	ISE Stock Exchange	Business Development Director

Chapter 1
Opening Address

Ian Domowitz

ROBERT SCHWARTZ: Ian Domowitz and I go way back, starting as professors together. Within a year of each other, we each made a big move in our academic careers – I went to Baruch, and Ian went to Penn State. Over the years, we have agreed on many things and have also disagreed many times. But as always, Professor Ian Domowitz's presentations and arguments are most interesting and very informative. You will not be disappointed today. Ian, my friend, welcome.

IAN DOMOWITZ: Thank you, Bob. As many of you know, Bob performs his magic every year. He manages to bring the right people to this conference, often at the most appropriate time. Not everybody may know that Bob is perhaps not just the father of market structure in the context of academic literature. He may actually be a grandfather! History plays a major role in anything that Bob brings to the table.

He called me up one day and said, I would really like you to speak at the conference this year on technology and regulation. I know that you can tie them together. As a matter of fact, you might even talk about technology and compliance. I replied, Bob, anything for you!

I recently attended a compliance conference. It was one of those 2-day affairs for compliance officers. In the entire conference booklet – that great phone book that has all the presentations and white papers – I found only one reference to technology. It was about e-mail retrieval systems. I figured that technology and compliance just do not seem to be connected, which brought me back to considering technology and regulation.

My first remarks are made with reference to Exhibit 1.1. We seem to agree on most everything these days. Electronic markets? Hey, we can check that box. It once was *the* hot topic of discussion. Buy-side empowerment? Technology, together with regulatory efforts, helped move execution activity to the buy-side, and they are taking responsibility for their trading and accountability for the outcome. Check that box. Best execution-based regulation? Best execution these days is not only a term; it is the cornerstone of principle-based regulation across the pond in terms of

I. Domowitz (✉)
Investment Technology Group Inc., New York, USA

R.A. Schwartz et al. (eds.), *Technology and Regulation: How Are They Driving Our Markets?*, Zicklin School of Business Financial Markets Series,
DOI 10.1007/978-1-4419-0480-5_1, © Springer Science+Business Media, LLC 2009

regulatory regimes, and it is heavily dependent upon technology. We are checking that box too. Virtual liquidity consolidation? I remember coming to these conferences in the past, and constantly hearing the word, "fragmentation." We are starting to hear it again, except in a new context: the vendors of liquidity are now "fragmented." But the market is not fragmented as some think, simply because these firms have used technology within current regulatory rules, and have done the free-market thing. They have basically connected everybody in a way that has consolidated pools of liquidity. Check that box.

If we agree on so much, do we actually agree on the nature of the interaction between technology and regulation? Or, as I used to tell my students, is the business of trading becoming more like the trading business? Are the lines becoming blurred? Do we tend to agree about where the business side meets the trading side? This is where regulation and technology meet. It was not always like that. The Exhibit 1.2 contains a few examples.

Some of you no doubt remember Leo Melamed. Melamed is a bit of a visionary out of Chicago. He is best known as the father of financial futures. The CFTC organized the very first conference in 1977 on the topic of trading automation and exchange automation. The conference was about bringing technology to the trading floor. Leo Melamed spoke. He felt so strongly about the topic that he wrote an article for the *Hofstra Law Review*, summarizing the talk. His speech argued against

---

☑ Electronic markets

☑ Buy side empowerment

☑ Best Execution based regulation

☑ Virtual liquidity consolidation

- If we agree on so much, do we also agree on the nature of the interaction between regulation and technology?

  or

- Have the lines between the trading business and the business of trading blurred so much that the issue becomes irrelevant?

Exhibit 1.1 An Agenda of Agreement?

- Leo Melamedand the 1977 CFTC automation conference

- European derivatives terminals appear in Chicago

- Reg ATS and 30 years of rule-making proposals

- The 1975 "National Market System,"ITS, and the sustainability of multiple exchange venues

---

Exhibit 1.2 A Few Provocative Events in the Intersection of Regulation and Technology

the automation of exchanges. He claimed that it was contrary to the very spirit of our regulatory framework. Now, Leo is also known as the father of something else – the Globex trading system. Globex currently is handling the majority of contract volume. It is a fully automated exchange. One could say that Melamed eventually came around in his thinking.

I like the next point on the slide. This is my chance to say that I have a crystal ball, since, just today, we have the news of the Eurex and ISE merger. A few years ago, all of a sudden, 26 terminals for the electronic trading of derivatives through the DTB appeared in Chicago. This caused an incredible furor. Technology had made it possible to bring the contracts to another city and to trade overseas. Who was going to regulate this trading? This became a big issue. The CFTC made a decision to permit trading. The 26 terminals were installed. Whether or not it was because of this, both the Board of Trade and the CME saw a decrease in their market share. In response, they lobbied the CFTC to rescind the permission for these terminals to be installed. The issue split the CFTC and the Commission itself. Finally, the matter got resolved. Now someone (Eurex) is actually entering through a purchase (of ISE). Globalization through automation of markets arrives, approved by US regulators.

With Reg ATS, we finally had regulation that covered the automation of the markets. Reg ATS brought technology and regulation together. You must realize how long that took. In 1969, the original Instinet was formed. You think about Instinet being born in the 1980s, right? It was indeed an SEC No-Action letter in 1986 that really got things rolling. But the very first Concept Release from the SEC, proposing regulation for automated electronic markets, came in 1969. It was motivated by the appearance of Instinet on the scene. It was voted up, and it was voted down, several times. Thirty years passed before we got to Reg ATS.

There were four separate major rule filings. There were many No-Action letters for the various market participants. That is because people did not know how to regulate a market that looked like an exchange but operated as a dealer. At the time, the regulatory language did not permit an electronic market to operate as an exchange. Consequently, technology and regulation were coming together in a contentious fashion. Concurrently, the language used to regulate trading markets was changing.

We witnessed rule filings and controversy for 30 years! Finally, there was Reg NMS, which is not a new term. The term dates back to the 1970s, a time when we had some ideas of a "national market system" and trade-through rules. We then set up something called ITS, the Intermarket Trading System. ITS first came to light in 1978, as an enabler of regulatory intent with respect to trade-throughs. I do believe that it may finally have gone the way of the dodo bird as private networks have now come on line.

Historically, the nexus between technology and regulation has been fraught with controversy. You can debate what came first, technology or regulation, when the two are linked in some fashion. Regardless, let me present some potentially contentious ideas, more consistent with the history I have cited than with an era of general agreement.

Here is my first thought. Technology is simply a legal safe harbor for regulation. We are starting to see demands for what is called best execution, for example. I have been with boards of directors of mutual funds that wanted to talk about best execution, and how to measure it. There was only one problem: no one knew what best execution meant. Although trustees love to talk about low commission rates, best execution is a qualitative standard for doing well. Best execution finds definition through process, as opposed to price. Define the process through technology, with its associated audit trail, and the safe harbor is established.

Which brings me to the empowerment of the buy-side. Where is it coming from in this view of the trading world? There is a lot of pressure on the trading desks to do something to achieve best execution. This something is the ship to the safe harbor of electronic trading. Why? We now have electronic execution. It is relatively easy to do. It operates with strategies that are well-defined with an eye towards achieving best execution in an increasingly complex world. This is what safe harbors are ultimately all about. You can measure performance because everything goes through order management systems and through trading algorithms. The buy-side is actually taking control of the trade.

There is one problem with this view of the world. You get corollaries that not everybody might agree with. The main corollary today concerns Reg NMS: it is a non-event. A safe harbor was already in place and people have fled there. We consider this next with reference to Exhibit 1.3.

Industry practitioners have looked closely at what happened to commission structures, from about 2003 through 2006, as trading became more electronic and moved away from the sell-side to the buy-side desks. This movement cost the sell-side about $4.7 billion in commissions over this period of time. By any stretch of the imagination, that is a lot of money. That is the pro-forma difference between what trading would look like today in terms of commissions, if the trading world had not changed since roughly 2003. That is our first data point.

The second data point is how big institutional commissions are in the United States. I have no idea what it is globally. But, there is agreement that overall it is in the order of $12 billion in the US markets. Maybe $13 billion. Now, let us ask, how

---

- The shift to the safe harbor is estimated to have cost $4.7 billion in commissions*

- Total U.S. annual commission pool is estimated at between $12 billion and $13 billion depending on source**

- Total industry spend on Reg NMS over a two year period is estimated to be $91 million***

- Reg NMS 'compliant'
    Firms that are serious about electronic trading have little to do
    Electronic trading is not an 'unintended consequence' of the new regulations, as has been claimed by some

---

*Bernstein Research
**Bernstein Research and the Tabb Group
***The Tabb Group

Exhibit 1.3 Regulation NMS as a Non-Event

much money is being spent on technology for the introduction of Reg NMS? Recall my earlier comment about the compliance packet, and the fact that there was scant information in it about technology. How much money will Reg NMS cost? I do not know if Larry Tabb is here today. But I looked at his survey data. This survey estimated that $91 million would be spent on Reg NMS over 2 years. That is roughly $45 million a year. Compare that to $12 billion in commissions. Even on Wall Street, I would say that $45 million relative to $12 billion is not a lot of spending. In other words, we are in the safe harbor.

Yet, everybody and their proverbial cousin quotes NMS for anything they want to do right now. The marketing people on Wall Street are no different. Reg NMS compliance is a big buzzword. What does compliance really mean? It is about technology being compliant with regulation. It is being used in marketing pitches. Except that we are already compliant. It cost the trading markets $4.7 billion in commissions, remember? Some claim that the electronic markets are an unintended consequence of Reg NMS. I do not agree. It is easier to buy into the idea that the regulatory authorities were smart enough to anticipate the safe harbor reaction. They threatened everybody with Reg NMS to get the entire industry to move. It worked.

I want to go back to my comments about language and Reg ATS. In doing so I will make reference to Exhibit 1.4. When I was in academia, I made a little money on the side as a consultant. One of my most memorable consulting engagements was a pro bono job for the SEC. One day I walked into a room filled with 14 lawyers to talk about what basically we now know as Reg ATS. The lawyers said, "We want to talk to you because we no longer have language to describe what is going on. Therefore, we are having trouble writing regulations that will capture the movement and technology for the automatic market relative to what was envisioned, back in

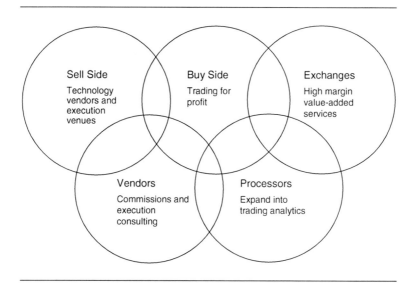

Exhibit 1.4   Technology and the Loss of Regulatory Language

the '40s." I submit that we are in the exact same situation today when it comes to regulation and technology. Except that now it is even worse.

Let me put this in context. We talk about the trading industry in terms of segments. We talk about the buy-side, the sell-side, exchanges, processors, and vendors. Why do we talk about the industry that way? Can you say that it is all legacy? That it is convenience? Actually, that is not quite true. We talk about it that way in large part because the regulators put us here when they wrote the regulation that underpins what we do today. They invented this structure. They regulated investment firms. We called them the buy-side. They regulated brokers and dealers in a different way. We called them the sell-side.

Exchanges have separate regulations, and the very term, "exchange" has regulatory significance. Processors are separately regulated, and vendors do what they want. I am not sure that back in the 1930s and 1940s the regulators understood the idea of technology as we understand it today.

I would say that these distinctions will become irrelevant. Technology will put us there. As the terminology becomes irrelevant, regulation must change, since regulation is essentially about law, and laws depend on definitions. New rules will have to accommodate changes in current terminology, in much the same way as the regulators had to write Reg ATS to resolve the distinction between exchanges and broker-dealers.

We see the blurring between segments on the sell-side and on the buy-side. What is the sell-side reaction, for example? The sell-side has become technology vendors. They are not trading any more. They set up execution venues. That sounds like exchanges to me. On the buy-side, I actually had a real rude shock. One day I walked into a very large buy-side shop and I was peppered with questions about how to do high-frequency trading for profit. Well, that is not exactly what I think of in terms of portfolio management; it sounds more like sell-side proprietary trading. The exchanges, on the other hand, are really getting into the idea of a high margin, value-added service. That is where the sell-side's profits come from.

As the exchanges get away from their mutual structure and become de-mutualized and for-profit, they are moving right in there. The vendors have discovered commissions. They have discovered the power of commissions and execution consulting. They are moving into sell-buy businesses. The processors? Processors are trying to get into trading analytics. They also need to broaden what they do. There are lots of reasons for this. Whether everybody is competing with one another, making deals with one another, or partnering with one another, it does not really matter. Technology has enabled all of this. Technology is what is really being swapped back and forth. Technology is the root of the regulatory problem.

As technology enables these distinctions to go away, regulatory language also goes away. Lawyers live by definitions. If you take away the definitions, the regulations must change. Let me give you a good example.

I saw a quote by Craig Donahue[1] not so long ago. He said that the competitive environment is not characterized as a battle between exchanges. Rather, it is a battle between the exchanges and the brokers. Did you know that, as late as 1998 in a

---

[1]Mr. Donahue is CEO of the Chicago Mercantile Exchange.

"This is not a battle between exchanges. The real battle is the exchanges...against the broker-dealers."

Craig Donohue, CME, March 16, 2007

Broker-Dealer Model	Exchange Model
• Trade execution	• Trade execution
• DMA products	• Proprietary workstations
• Analytical trading tools	• Analytical trading tools
• Information services	• Data provider
• Trading strategies	• Expanded order types
• Capital commitment	• Liquidity
• Connectivity	• Linkages

Exhibit 1.5 Competition Between the Exchanges and the Broker-Dealers

Concept Release leading up to Reg ATS, the SEC had language that basically said that they did not believe that competition existed between the sell-side and the exchanges? But competition more than existed. All you had to do was to look outside of the United States years ago to see this.

Consider Exhibit 1.5, which I wrote years ago for a presentation in Brussels.

It was part of a broader effort to talk to the European Commission about the effects and implications of regulations when they were first being drafted. This was a big issue in Europe years ago. We are starting to face it today here. The entries in Exhibit 1.5 are broken down very crudely, I will admit. There is a broker-dealer model and there is an exchange model. The broker-dealers offer trade execution and so too do the exchanges. These days, the broker-dealers are all offering DMA products.

What is a DMA product? It is essentially a box that goes on your desk. It is part of the real estate on your desk that provides information, and that allows you to send orders to a variety of destinations. Well, the exchanges are doing this too. They call them *proprietary workstations*. Rumor has it that some are now investigating these things for floor brokers to route out to other places from the floor.

Analytical trading tools are now part of both types of organizations. That is a challenge. The notion is that content adds value and, therefore, can be used to support more high-margin business within the trading business. The earliest example was probably in Germany, which has been offering transactions cost analysis tools for years, a concept that is now popular with sell-side vendors.

We have a new move to create new value-added data by the exchanges. They see that simple distributions of the raw data will not be as profitable going forward. That has been realized elsewhere around the world for some time, although value-added trading data were traditionally the product of the sell-side shops.

The sell-side spends a great deal of effort these days developing and offering trading strategies. We call them algorithms. The funny thing is that exchanges have been doing it for a while. The exchange products are called *expanded order types.*

Trade strategies and order types are really the same thing. We see more of it in derivative exchanges than we do in equity exchanges. Look at LIFFE in London. As a user, you can get an entire Web page full of trading strategies. In the derivatives world, they call this market education. They are educating you on strategies the same way that the sell-side does.

Capital commitment. This is supposed to be the last of the pure sell-side roles. The exchanges have provided liquidity forever. Many of the arguments surrounding demutualization have to do with capital commitment. I have the feeling that they are more linked than people would like to admit.

Connectivity. The sell-side is part of the movement towards a safe harbor. The sell-side has been getting into the connectivity game by building systems or through acquisitions. Way back when, this was called "linkages" by the exchanges. Now they are calling it connectivity too, because, through Reg NMS, they actually have to route out.

These are two business models, broker-dealers and exchanges. They look the same to me. But they are regulated differently.

Regulatory language does not accommodate them, vis-à-vis the similarities. This is where technology and regulation will truly come together. We will see change in regulatory language and, therefore, in regulation due to technology. The change is altering the business model of these players who have been separated by their language and their practices. This was where my title line comes in: "Don't panic." Don't panic is a quote from the *Hitchhiker's Guide to the Galaxy.* Some of you may be familiar with it. There was a Hollywood movie version that shows people who run around the galaxy with this book. On the back cover in big capital letters it says, "DON'T PANIC."

Of course, in the Hollywood version, it concerns a guy in a bathrobe who is running around the galaxy constantly panicking, trying to make sure that he knows where his towel is! We are sort of in that boat right now. We should not panic. This is a natural set of events. I believe that rewriting the regulatory language will be a perfectly natural course of events. Maybe it will take another 30 years like Reg ATS did. I would hope not. But this is the type of thing that I believe we will be discussing today. As the panels come up here, you might keep this question in mind: how does one explain that an exchange really is a competitor? Or, that a broker-dealer is a competitor? This will change the world a little more than it already has today. With that, I thank you very much.

SCHWARTZ: I would like to give the audience a chance to ask Ian a question or two.

STEVE WUNSCH (ISE Stock Exchange) [From the Floor]: My question concerns the membership part. That person is going away – do you have any comments or thoughts about that?

DOMOWITZ: That is a different line of thought, but I can bring it back to technology. The argument has been made that demutualization was driven by technology in the first place. The notion was that a mutual structure was convenient and necessary when you have a trading floor that would only allow a certain number of people on the floor. In other words, it was only so big. So we developed mutual structures. People have made the argument that the advent of the automation of exchanges actually was a driving force behind getting everybody to move away from mutual structures that were not necessary by law. If you track demutualization since Stockholm (which was the first to demutualize), I believe you would find that no exchange that was not automated demutualized. At least in the early days of the game. That was the connection between demutualization, automation, and hence regulation.

UNIDENTIFIED SPEAKER [From the Floor]: What was the driving force for automation?

DOMOWITZ: There are a couple things. First of all it is not so much regional. Let me give you a data point. Between 1988 and 1992, 28 new derivatives exchanges were built globally. Twenty-six of them were fully automated. That came from an explosion back then in interest in plain vanilla derivatives. Then it calmed down. Now we have resurgence. All of that happened outside of the United States, though. The Chicago exchanges would send their diplomats to foreign countries to talk to other exchanges about adopting the floor model. But, at the end of the day, it was cost that drove people to automation when they put up new exchanges.

Therefore, you get this big influx of new exchanges, and retro fits, that basically had to deal with the cost structure of building one of these things. The Treasury bond market for Chicago cost $187 million to build. That was a floor to trade one instrument. The LSE had plans that allowed for $450 million to build their floor-based exchange, before they decided to go for an automated structure. But you can build an automated exchange, with all the bells and whistles, for less than $20 million. You can run it for 60% less. The economics are astounding. The answer to your question is that vested human capital, and financial interests in certain market segments, kept the trading floors alive, not the technology.

SCHWARTZ: Thank you ever so much Ian.

Chapter 2
The Impact of Electronic Trading Technology

Richard Holowczak, Leslie Boni, Kevin Callahan, Alfred Eskandar, James Leman, Robert McCooey, and Joseph Wald

ROBERT SCHWARTZ: Rich Holowczak is head of the Wasserman Trading Floor – Subotnick Center here at Baruch College. Rich is my colleague, a friend and also a co-author. Please welcome him.

RICHARD HOLOWCZAK: Thanks Bob. The professor in me wants to get some definitions out of the way. So, my first question for the panel is, what do you consider to be electronic trading technology? It was suggested that there is a distinction between tools and venues.

JOSEPH WALD: Electronic trading technology encompasses everything we have today in terms of market structure. It is the foundation upon which buyers and sellers can interact. It also accommodates various types of trades and instruments. The technology is so vast, so broad and interconnected, that there is no substitute for electronic trading in the equities or derivative markets. Certainly, it is far superior to a floor-based and less automated trading system.

HOLOWCZAK: Alfred?

ALFRED ESKANDAR: My CTO and my compliance officer are pretty nervous that I am talking at a conference about technology and regulation! The difference between tools and venues is a great place to start. Tools, such as a direct market access product, or an algorithm, get you to a venue like Liquidnet. The venue is where you ultimately execute and change an idea into a position.

HOLOWCZAK: Bob, how about a venue?

ROBERT MCCOOEY: I guess I am the venue guy. There are a small number of venues that you want to talk about as exchanges. But it seems that there are a lot of trading tools, which look more and more like venues. The lines continue to blur between tools and venues. Traditional venues, such as NASDAQ, are creating more tools to help our customers, especially our partners – large investment banks that are market makers in NASDAQ-listed stocks – to access displayed liquidity.

R. Holowczak (✉)
Zicklin School of Business, Baruch College, CUNY, New York, USA

R.A. Schwartz et al. (eds.), *Technology and Regulation: How Are They Driving Our Markets?*, Zicklin School of Business Financial Markets Series,
DOI 10.1007/978-1-4419-0480-5_2, © Springer Science+Business Media, LLC 2009

HOLOWCZAK: Let me pick up on something that Ian Domowitz hinted at earlier. It is sort of a chicken and egg scenario. Are we in the closing stages of a decade or more of regulations in our trading markets? Or is it the dawn of a new age of innovation that came about from that same regulation? Or does technology take us to a place where regulators are comfortable saying, let it be so?

LESLIE BONI: A couple of years ago I spent a year as a visiting scholar at the Office of Economic Analysis at the Securities and Exchange Commission. The SEC was thinking long and hard about Reg NMS,[1] and about how to respond to various concerns – in particular from frustrated retail investors. I had been one of those same retail investors. I was frustrated by placing a limit order through my broker, seeing myself getting traded through, wondering why my order did not get executed.

Reg NMS may have been inevitable. Technology has made so many advances that the NYSE hybrid was probably a foregone conclusion. I do not agree that Reg NMS is a non-event. I think the $91 million spending estimate on Reg NMS over 2 years, in the survey mentioned by Ian, is low. At UNX alone, we are spending millions to prepare for Reg NMS.

HOLOWCZAK: What are your thoughts, Jim?

JAMES LEMAN: As Bob mentioned there are three main drivers of innovation in the industry: technology, regulation, and competition. I would say that competition is probably the biggest driver. That said, we actually experienced the biggest industry changes when the equity bubble burst in the market break of 2000. Up until then, through the 1980s and 1990s, the markets were relatively stable, and so also was the profitability of trading. Of course, prior to 2000, we had decimalization, which narrowed the bid/ask spread. And electronic crossing mechanisms were introduced, which also impacted market making.

Yes, these events ate away at the profitability of traditional trading, but this was offset by growing trading volume in strong markets. Then the bubble burst. Suddenly, volume was drying up in a bearish market, so firms were earning less money on fewer trades. In other words, the bursting of the bubble resulted in far-reaching changes that traced their roots to events prior to 2000, and these changes were magnified by the market break.

Consequently, more changes occurred because of this market break than from earlier events, including the Y2K scare, preparation for European Monetary Union, and decimalization. Now, investment mangers, mutual funds and hedge funds realized it would be harder to make money in bear market conditions. The events prior to 2000 ultimately sowed the seed of what was to follow. Few could have imagined the layoffs and how revenue would be cut in half at some firms. The industry was forced to seek better ways to become more cost-efficient, using more advanced

---

[1]Regulation NMS, or National Market System, adopted by the SEC in April 2005, contains four separate but interrelated rules on order protection for trade-throughs, intermarket access, sub-penny trading and market data. The regulation was aimed at overhauling the regulatory structure of US equity markets.

technology and less trading professionals in a competitive market. Firms, in fact, started to look more closely at the cost of trading. That was a driver for a lot of the subsequent changes.

Regulation acts as an independent force. The trade-through rule is interesting. I was in the camp that believed that retail investors needed protection for their limit orders. That rule certainly helped them. But on television recently I noticed TD Waterhouse advertising how, if you placed an order through its online discount brokerage, it would guarantee you the absolute best execution. That means that they actually have to comply with Reg NMS, which promotes best execution.

But you must wonder about competition, about how online retail brokers could be legitimately competing on one level, and yet it was still possible that you would not get best execution. But there are times, perhaps even in the case of the trade-through rule, when regulation tries to accelerate the pace of change.

HOLOWCZAK: I was asked to give a presentation to MBA students about alternative trading systems. I started on 5–10 and I ended up with 56 ATSs – and just kept going! So how is technology being used to reach those pools of liquidity, and to give the trader a more consistent view of the market?[2]

LEMAN: We are seeing creativity in the trading process, as the goals of the business side are accomplished by technology. In this regard, Exchanges, to a certain extent, have been at the forefront in the US. The exchanges' mechanisms for creating new order types and memberships might have been considered rigid in the past. The traditional stock exchanges had very straightforward orders handled by human beings.

As technology opened the door, the protocols evolved. Now we have Reserve Orders and other order types. The NYSE acquired the all-electronic Archipelago and has the hybrid on the floor. NASDAQ has a crossing mechanism. Industry people designed new and innovative systems. That is where they stepped ahead of the regulators.

We are in a period of experimentation. There are numerous pools trying to achieve the perfect model to provide more liquidity and more transparency, at the same time protecting against a certain amount of information leakage. You see that in the different ETFs where one size no longer fits all. For example, certain ETFs are aimed at the retail investor.[3]

---

[2] Dark pools, electronic networks that match buyers and sellers anonymously, accounted for some 10% of daily trading volume in the US, as of May 2008, compared with just under 1% in 2003. Overall, dark pools account for the major share of the total individual ATSs mentioned by the speaker. There were 42 such dark pools altogether, with brokerage firms sending them 17% of their equity trades in this period. That is forecast to grow to about 20% by 2010. At the same time, the average trade size was 260 shares during this same period, compared to 1,400 shares a decade earlier. Among the top dark pools, Goldman Sachs Sigma X averaged 60.03 million shares daily in March 2008; Credit Suisse CrossFinder averaged 54.3 million while Liquidnet had 33.1 million (estimates and company data, adjusted for double-counting of volume.) Source: *Wall Street Journal*, May 08, 2008, "Dark Pools" Being Spoiled by Success: Glut Dims Their Allure for Big Traders.

[3] The relatively low cost and the tax advantages of Exchange Traded Funds, which invest in a variety of investments, including gold, currencies, commodities and equities, has attracted increasing interest from retail investors. All told, 634 ETFs traded on US exchanges in February 2008, compared 432 a year earlier, according to the Investment Company Institute. Assets totaled $559 billion.

The experimental process will determine who has the most successful ATS model. I see some ATSs combining until we get to that point. It is not a slam-dunk. Small-cap stocks might be active in one ATS, for instance, while another attracts large-cap stocks. Algorithmic traders may find yet another ATS more attractive. In the past, regulators could not be proactive because they did not understand the trading business well enough. When they came across a rule violation, or found an electronic-related practice that was brought to their attention because of a complaint – a "for-cause" examination – that is when they would focus most closely on some aspect of electronic trading. But the regulators were behind the pace of change.

Now participants are using technology to create new venues, but they do not always think about the in-house compliance people when they start. This is not productive. On the other hand, in some houses today the compliance people are involved in the development process of new technological systems.

BONI: I also agree that there is a fascinating experiment going on with the various trading systems, and with the many different fragmented places where you can trade. I would think that competitive forces would quickly sort that out. My guess is that we do not need a dozen different pools of liquidity.

LEMAN: I predict that the regulators will stand aside. Perhaps they will not allow the marketplace to truly define what it wants. But because of its stand, it might nudge regulation in one direction or another. In an historic regulatory context, the interesting thing is that, in the old days, when we had paper tickets and manual processing, it was very difficult to construct a comprehensive timeline of the trade execution, and to gather information and order-entry data after a certain point in the process.

Today, you essentially have an electronic time stamp of each trade, in addition to the associated rules, which include Reg NMS. This means that compliance departments now pay more attention to all the decisions made by traders. After all, there is an abundance of data electronically collected, which allows regulators to draw more inferences. Consequently, you can now get more refined transaction-cost analysis than ever before.

Under the old manual system, it was very difficult to reconstruct the trade details past a certain point in the transaction. Regulators, for example, can now better track step-outs, including the executing brokers and the underlying security details. Today, with all this data gathering, every compliance officer has become skittish. Every regulator has a rich field of historical information to see what was done in the market, inside the four walls of the broker-dealer. That is the defining factor going forward.

MCCOOEY: I agree with Jim. That is one of the big challenges – the fact that trading is purely science and no longer art. I am referring to the evolution of the trading markets over the last decade, with the creation and growth of ECNs and other alternatives venues. The buy-side trader gained more direct control of his or her order, starting primarily in NASDAQ-listed issues through the late 1990s, and the early part of this decade. At the New York Stock Exchange, market structure had prevented the buy-side from directly accessing this market, even as the buy-side enjoyed more control over their orders on NASDAQ. In the end, the buy-side eventually prevailed at the Big Board, because of pressure from competitive venues like Island ECN, and frustration by the SEC at the slow pace of change at the NYSE.

The customer now controls the order. Regulation has two challenges: manpower and understanding. The markets have moved so quickly, and technology has advanced so far, that the number of people it takes, and their understanding of how to regulate this market, is growing tremendously. They will need to understand the markets when they look at the buy-side and the sell-side. With fragmented markets and now the execution obligations, it is a far more challenging environment for the regulators.

ESKANDAR: The different ATSs that have sprung up in the last 12–18 months are like different flavors of different types of trading. There are not a lot of meaningful differences among them. A good question is, what, ultimately, is going to last? What, ultimately, delivers value? The pendulum has swung so heavily to the buy-side that all these different things are coming out now. Let me see if I can satisfy them with the new buy-side trader's appetite, offering large quant trading, between these hours, or, a continuous cross model, or another model with additional features. Ultimately, the ones who survive will be the ones that have the greatest effect.

WALD: The 24 million-dollar question is, how much liquidity is there in all these different pools? And, is it actionable liquidity, or just potential liquidity – that is, orders just sitting on somebody's desk? Whatever the case, is liquidity being heavily underestimated?

These markets are now electronic. The model has changed from having an outside sell-side trader take the order from the buy-side, to having the buy-side take the order, break it into smaller pieces, and then enter the pieces over time into the marketplace. Now, having the ability to put that reserve order in some type of dark pool, we can see that actionable liquidity has grown dramatically.

Now we will ask where the liquidity is, and use algorithms to go out there, trying to consolidate all of these different liquidity pools. There is no information leakage in the dark pools, which helps to minimize market impact. That, in addition to the technology to maximize connectivity – the ability to be in multiple dark pools at the same time, and to adapt to where the liquidity is in a very quick time frame – is contributing to the growth in actionable liquidity.

One of the big challenges that we face is making it work. Will we find liquidity on the other side? Will there be anything to execute against? What we found was actually remarkable: 28.9% of all executed trades done through these consolidated algorithms actually got done in dark pools of liquidity. The number is mind-boggling. In truth, this new, actionable liquidity gives us an ability that was never there before – the ability to trade in size.

ESKANDAR: There is a streaming ATS facilitating smaller order flow passing through as it tries to hit a residing large block. This phenomenon is the newest trend. Ultimately, more ATSs will move towards that model. I would categorize Liquidnet's H2O, UBS's PIN and Millennium as streaming ATSs. In this model, a large block order will reside in the system while small passive orders nip at it. It is the right way to execute a large order that wants to be passive. Rather than the large order going out to the market and putting artificial pressure on the price – demanding too much size that is not available – the order just sits back because it is passive. And it soaks up the liquidity.

This works, of course, only if you have enough liquidity to satisfy the order. The other type of model is for the illiquid, difficult to trade names. In fact, if you look at our statistics and opinions we are 42% of the block volume on average for difficult to trade names. If you go down further to the micro-cap level, 100% of the block volume gets done in one print on our system. This does not happen in every name, but as the liquidity grows it becomes more prevalent.

LEMAN: Will technology allow you to break this down into a security-by-security decision of how to trade? With the drive towards more detailed analysis and the empowerment offered by the computer, the reality is that we have more choices of liquidity pools. For example, there is an ATS that requires a minimum share order size of 25,000 shares; another allows the trader to determine the size of the block and search for orders in multiple venues. The trader could also select an ATS suitable for passive orders, the type of orders that add liquidity to a system but do not match when they are entered into a continuous order matching system. That is part of what Alfred is driving at. Whether your trading intentions are passive, aimed at trading in a periodic system once a day, or you are using a streaming ATS facility, you do not want to disclose any trading information to the market. The leakage of information continues to be a very important concern to the buy-side.

The other trend seems to be the continuing decline of commission rates. We are seeing the evolution of more proprietary trading by certain market players who are trying to offset their other revenue losses. An appetite for this seems to be emerging on the sell-side. So we will continue to see a customization of certain types of securities trading, mainly in dark pools. Exchanges and dark pools will also offer services as market consultants on transaction-cost analysis, that is services that analyze trade flows for customers. It is a way for these market players to distinguish themselves. In the past, transaction-cost analysis was offered by third-party vendors, but in the new environment exchanges will step into this space to show customers the cost and other advantages of sending them their trades.

MCCOOEY: Richard, in the midst of this change, there are still some very, very large players in the market, including NASDAQ. We are still in the high 40% in terms of our market share. We are also 16–17% of New York Stock Exchange securities that are matched in our book everyday. We are also seeing over 40% of the Big Board traffic go through our book every single day. A tremendous amount of liquidity – more and more each day – is still resident at the New York Stock Exchange and at NASDAQ.

BONI: I ask this because we have great success finding liquidity at NASDAQ. Do you guys publish what percent of the NASDAQ volume is hidden?

MCCOOEY: I do not believe that we give it out.

BONI: Maybe you should!

MCCOOEY: It is a large percentage. I would prefer to have Frank Hatheway answer that question.

BONI: But you get liquidity in your market. If you just told us what that liquidity was you might get more of it.

MCCOOEY: I will take that under advisement!

HOLOWCZAK: I want to bring the human being back for a moment. Then maybe we can get rid of him again. The question is, how is the role of the trader changing in the face of all this technology? On the one hand, we have all these algorithms and trading decisions that can be made. Maybe computers can make them. But for the computers to do this, some human being would have to sit down and pour through that micro-level data before it is entered into a computer as a trading program. Again, the question is, how will the role of the trader evolve? Will we see a day when the trade goes right from the portfolio manager to the market without any other human intervention?

MCCOOEY: My little quote was, "algos, algos everywhere, and not a person to think." That ends up being something of a problem. Going back to what we talked about earlier – the art vs. science of trading – I do believe in the art of trading because I grew up on the trading floor. I moved to the science of trading by working at NASDAQ. I understand that the two of them need to be combined in a way that provides best execution. When we are talking about tools and venues, we are talking about trying to find liquidity. I spent my entire career dealing with the institutional buy-side. I understand their need to get as much liquidity as they possibly can without moving the price, without having market impact.

So we need to think that algorithms are a great tool. All the trading innovations and rules are wonderful because they help us to find liquidity. Nevertheless, it has to be people who think about how trading is done. People are needed to analyze the trading. I have always worried about that from a trading perspective, as the number of trading professionals on the sell-side has decreased.

More and more of the buy-side are using algorithmic trading. I was on a trading desk this past Thursday when one fellow got three orders from his portfolio manager. He literally clicked and sent the three of them to big shops using an algo. He said, "Isn't this great!" In about 8 min he had bought 42,600 shares out of his 50,000-share order. And the portfolio manager walked into the room and said, "Oh, how's everyone?" Frankly, I do not know why the portfolio manager could not do that trade himself. So, unless there is value added by that buy-side or sell-side intermediary, there is a chance that more of these trading jobs will disappear.[4]

---

[4]The elimination of trading jobs continued at a rapid pace after the conference as cost-efficiencies and automation reduced headcount. In an interview in May 2008 with Reuters, NYSE CEO Duncan Niederauer, said the Big Board was seriously looking at closing the so-called Garage and moving the remaining floor traders into the Main Room. The exchange had previously shut three of the five trading rooms, as job cuts thinned the ranks of the NYSE floor. The total number of people on the floor reportedly shrank to about 2,100 from 3,000, over several months just prior to this conference. "On trading desks, the human factor has been replaced with more and better algorithms," said Robert McCooey, in a subsequent response to a question for this book. "Those left seem to fall into just a few categories: those with strong client relationships, those involved with risk management, and those who know how the systems actually work." This former top NYSE floor broker added: "I think that the proverbial pendulum has swung way too far, and I have heard frequent complaints from the buy-side about the lack of service and attention from the sell-side. With all the layoffs, the bandwidth to provide this service does not exist."

HOLOWCZAK: Kevin, what do you think?

KEVIN CALLAHAN: The role of the trader is changing significantly. It is becoming more strategic in the overall investment process. In the old days, you handed the order to a clerk to give the ticket to one of the big banks to trade. Now the trader and the trade function are becoming strategic. If you want to look at where that is taking place, look at the hedge funds

I am thinking of a hedge fund that had 10 billion dollars under management. They had 26 people at that firm with the title of trader. I looked at a mutual fund that has over 500 billion dollars under management. The fund had fewer than 16 people with the title of trader. So the hedge funds think of themselves as traders first, and as portfolio managers second. Most of the hedge funds are not heavily regulated, and they are focused on making money. They recognize that the trader is part of an integral process of making a lot of money, of producing returns.

However, there are sell-side prop desks – and some enormous, sophisticated, highly quantitative hedge funds – that want nothing more than to trade for the money management industry, with the minimum amount of traders, using algorithms to send their orders directly to the market. In prop trading like this, the trader is well versed in advanced electronic trading, and is becoming more strategic in the trading process. If you look at the part of this industry where the most competition and innovation is happening, they value the trader very, very much. They want to empower that trader. That role will become ever more important.

HOLOWCZAK: Joe?

WALD: New roles are being created to support these newly empowered traders on the buy-side who are embracing electronic trading and related tools, such as algorithms and direct market access, along with high-touch trading services, from the sell-side. These roles include the liquidity strategist on different products. These liquidity strategists, as they are called, work with our clients to help them better understand how these tools and services can be deployed, since each client needs to use them efficiently and effectively sourcing liquidity.

Some of our liquidity strategists on staff are former traders who are knowledgeable about market structure and electronic trading. Like execution consultants, they work with clients on pairing up a trading objective of a client, with achieving a best execution or trading benchmark target through, say, a particular algorithm, or some other customized offering. These liquidity strategists and execution consultants are critical in helping the transition take place in terms of empowering the buy-side trader. That is probably the most critical shift that we are seeing in terms of the new sophistication in trading tools. The coaches are there to help traders maximize the tools that they have.

HOLOWCZAK: Leslie?

BONI: We have a lot of hedge fund clients. Those traders continue to ask for more sophisticated tools. That is the great thing about technology. It used to be that the New York Stock Exchange had to close on Wednesday, and that did not end until computers came along that enabled the NYSE to open on Wednesdays and boost efficiency. Similarly, we are seeing electronic trading tools, direct market access tools, better algos, and smart routing tools, all helping the trader. What you have is a sort of arms race. Typically, our clients want to know what we can offer them that will be better than everybody else has. It is all about technology.

HOLOWCZAK: James?

LEMAN: The skill set of the traders will change substantially. The impact of derivative instruments – and how they trade in harmony with the cash market – will become more pronounced. The use of quantitative techniques, mathematical skills, and the ability to interplay these two will make the pure cash trader more of a novelty than in the past.

In the old days – up until about 15 years ago in the US, a decade ago in Europe – there were no separate buy-side desks. In fact, in many instances in Europe today, the portfolio managers still do their own trading. Historically, the portfolio manager would pick the stocks and also send the orders for execution. Eventually, there was a division of labor with buy-side traders doing nothing but handle orders. They operated separately from portfolio managers who did not think that trading was something they should do. Perhaps they thought that trading was too pedestrian. In Europe, this change occurred a short while later than in the US, as the market was becoming more complex here and assets were growing.

The ability to go back to that arrangement – with portfolio managers handling their own trading – is essentially being facilitated today by technology. In some instances, asset managers seeking better returns to hedge funds, or engaging complex strategies, are handling the orders themselves. So, the tendency will be a demand for more sophisticated traders.

The type of professionals who will succeed will need different skills than the ones who are there now. The professionals on trading desks on the broker side, and more than likely on the buy-side, will need more quantitatively oriented skills. They will need more understanding of derivative products and derivatives pricing and risk management, and more familiarity with electronic tools. There are going to be multiple products available for trading. Traders will not just be trading equities, but equities and derivatives of equities, and potentially foreign exchange because there will be more trading across borders – on the buy-side and the sell-side.

With direct market access today, brokers are providing front-end interfaces, or tools, so that the buy-side trader can pull the trigger on the trade, or use a pass-through mechanism, which means that the trade is not touched by a broker. There will still be buy-side firms that want the broker to handle the trade, but there will be other customers who want the broker to give them the pipe that electronically goes to the different destinations, so that they can pull the trigger and handle the trades themselves. In some instances you do not have that, so the division of the market must be embraced.

HOLOWCZAK: Any questions?

UNIDENTIFIED SPEAKER [From the Floor]: The broker-dealers are now automated and happen to have ATS licenses. But I am not sure that there is competition in this space. Traders are screaming about liquidity. But, where is the competition?

MCCOOEY: There is tremendous competition. For instance, NASDAQ is rolling out its Intraday Cross. Then there is a venue, which recently started to exclude sell-side brokers from their crosses. As a result, several brokers moved their orders from this venue over to our Intraday Cross.[5] Every change in market structure creates new sets of opportunities and fosters more competition.

UNIDENTIFIED SPEAKER [From the Floor]: I can definitely attest to that. It feels that we spent the better part of the last year connecting to a different cross every single week. There is tremendous competition, and the way that liquidity is being moved around has people trying different venues. There is a very robust, varied menu of competition out there for these dark pools.

ESKANDAR: This just reminded me of the bold, fragmented ATS and execution venue community. These dozens of different ATS flavors may offer something unique, but chances are they will not deliver. At the end of the day you guys – the buy-side – want size. You know, you are interested in reducing opportunity costs. You are interesting in not missing any trades. You are interested in reducing your market impact. All of these things have high value. High value comes at a price. A lot of times one share is sort of contrasted to another share. Executing a hundred shares of IBM is not the same as executing 100 shares of Telarian, or something else that is not frequently traded.

The buy-side is already deciding which venue to go to based on liquidity, value and price. Before any trade goes up in any particular venue, all these things have been considered. The buy-side trader selects his venues before he trades a stock. That choice is based on the value that he places on each venue. If these venues have the same value proposition, they should be pricing equally for their services.

WALD: And if different venues come in and compete, that will obviously drive prices to a different level.

CALLAHAN: Moreover, we are still in the early stages of the analysis of execution quality on the buy-side. The buy-side still uses many brokers because of the other ancillary services that they provide, often paid for via soft-dollar arrangements. As unbundling evolves, and as commission sharing arrangements gain ground, more people will be moving to the pure execution venues, and fewer people will go to a broker simply because he is offering a range of other stuff. But that will have to evolve.

The real problem is that buy-side people have different approaches to their goals. Some market participants, for example, might like a certain kind of order. Some ATSs apparently favor the buy-side, because the sell-side does not make the commitment to be there first. There is very little leakage on some ATSs. The customer may be most interested in a mid-point print. So, the end user wants more

---

[5] NASDAQ launched the Intraday Cross and Post-Close Cross on June 5, 2007. Earlier, NASDAQ introduced the Opening and Closing Crosses and IPO/Halt Cross. McCooey later identified the unnamed venue in his comments as ITG's POSIT, which prior to the conference began excluding sell-side brokers from its crosses.

analysis of what each system offers. Why is one ATS better than another? How do they impact best execution responsibilities? There is no comprehensive definition of best execution. It will get more and more refined.

HOLOWCZAK: Bill Freund?

BILL FREUND (Pace University) [From the Floor]: You see a vast number of mergers in the industry. I wonder to what extent that is driven by electronic sales, and to what extent it is driven by reducing excess capacity in the industry. What other factors might be involved?

HOLOWCZAK: Jim?

LEMAN: One of the driving forces at the New York Stock Exchange – and we now see others doing it – is the creation of new products, such as derivatives, that have a certain amount of stickiness. That is why the NYSE bought Euronext, and why it is getting into options and bought Archipelago. Equities, by their nature, can trade in multiple places that do not have to have to have an allegiance to an exchange. Futures contracts, on the other hand, are generally much less portable, because the futures contract and its settlement mechanism locks the customer into the clearing-house that is associated with the exchange. That is why the Chicago Mercantile Exchange has such a lock on the futures contracts that trade there. That is why its market capitalization and revenue stream is well protected. You can trade an NYSE stock anywhere in the world, and clear and settle it. So the NYSE as a demutualized business needs to have products that are stickier. It needs a revenue steam that cannot be erased as easily by outside competition.

If the standardization of accounting rules for European and US securities takes place, that will accelerate the ability to trade securities across borders. Right now the US markets – the NYSE and NASDAQ – have been shunned by many listed companies in favor of London to avoid regulatory reporting requirements in the US; and accounting rules and disclosure rules here – GAPP and Sarbanes-Oxley[6] – that are viewed as more severe than non-US standards in the minds of companies in Europe.

Exchanges are becoming for profit-organizations with diverse product lines that generate revenue. Whether or not they associate themselves with the clearing process of derivatives, the sale of market data, or the ability to offer derivative products across different countries, their aim is to link, as much as possible, to different exchanges. The International Securities Exchange came out with an announcement about that shortly before this whole thing took off with Deutsche Boerse.

I would expect Singapore, Hong Kong and other markets to become attractive targets in tapping institutional money in those markets. Exchanges want to attract flow in whatever form it takes. They want to export the order flow from those parts of the world back to the home markets. This will link derivative markets, cash markets and their clearing organizations, as we have never seen before.

---

[6] GAPP is the acronym for Generally Accepted Accounting Principles. The Sarbanes-Oxley Act of 2002, enacted in response to corporate scandals at Enron, Tyco and other companies, established stricter standards for public companies and accounting firms in the US.

ESKANDAR: At the end of the day, you will see tremendous technology that will permit you to trade across multiple markets and borders.

WALD: To follow up on the opportunities that MFID represents, let me say that I have always thought that the US market was the incubator for a lot of capital market change. Even though it is not exactly emulated in other parts of the world, it will be followed. And it is happening in other products, such as options and futures. I would have to say that Europe is next, followed by Asia in terms of market experimentation.

UNIDENTIFIED SPEAKER [From the Floor]: What would you advise an issuer? Let's take investment bankers out of here for a minute and talk about stocks. Issuers have a lot of problems now with their share prices. What would you counsel them or advise them with respect to listing? They feel they have no control over the price of their stock.

MCCOOEY: The issuers will never have control over the price of their stock.

UNIDENTIFIED SPEAKER [From the Floor]: I am really asking if an auction process, or what we saw Google and others do, is the wave of the future?

MCCOOEY: In terms of an IPO?

UNIDENTIFIED SPEAKER [From the Floor]: Yes.

MCCOOEY: There are a number of factors – in the way you list and why you list on a certain venue. In the NASDAQ model, the issuer pays NASDAQ a fee, and NASDAQ provides the issuer with a set of services. The New York Stock Exchange has a different model. You pay the NYSE and the specialist is supposed to provide you with some fuzzy services. An issuer should think about liquidity. More and more liquidity is residing in the NASDAQ book every day. That is one of the things we talk about to issuers.

WALD: Your investment bankers would probably talk to you about your company and its distribution of presumed ownership, your customer base, and so on. In the US market, whether you select two of the classic players – the NYSE and NASDAQ – or a smaller player, your securities will trade in a more liquid form with a lot more dispersion today because of Reg NMS. Will you also risk trading your securities in another form in European markets? Will you consider trading derivatives on the same market in any form? If so, you are getting, presumably, a more sophisticated market mechanism for your securities.

We see people with option programs for their corporate executives. For example, Google will permit these people to trade those options in some form. The diversity of where you want your securities to list will be a moot point eventually because, within the next 5 or 6 years, they will trade around the world anyway. Technology will allow people to trade a security in different time zones, perhaps in different currencies. It will be a global game.

CALLAHAN: For the first time in history, we have seen a net outflow of public equity in this country. The smaller issuers can argue that some of these regulations in the US, such as Sarbanes-Oxley, are limiting small companies' ability to go public here.

On another front, you have all this private equity money coming in and taking companies private. We have less public equity available today than we did a year ago. In this context, what we do for issuers, including providing sufficient liquidity in their stocks for trading, is very important.

The NYSE specialists had a relationship with the issuers. The specialists were responsible for providing liquidity in the stocks that were assigned to them. As markets become more electronic and you have virtual market makers – we have several of them now – none of them really has a responsibility to those issuers to actually provide liquidity. They are acting essentially on an agency basis and not making markets.

There have been some experiments in Europe in this regard, where the issuer can actually pay a market maker to help provide and find liquidity. That is something that we should look at in this country as markets become more electronic. A lot of these little companies will suffer if nobody steps up and helps them. Perhaps we should empower the issuer to be able to pay the market maker to help with its stock. This might strengthen market structure. This might provide market makers and specialists with another incentive to provide liquidity. That arrangement could turn out to be most important in the trading of less liquid stocks, and in volatile and difficult market conditions.

HOLOWCZAK: We have time for one more question.

ANDREW SMALL (Scottrade, Inc.) [From the Floor]: On the proliferation of ATSs and dark pools, there are certain perceptions that secret markets are being created with the proliferation of ATSs and dark pools. Is that an accurate perception?

ESKANDAR: That perception is the result of calling them dark pools rather than non-displayed markets. The word dark is sinister and evil. Dark implies something bad. Dark pools, or whatever you want to call them, have a tremendous value when they work. The value is basically in offering the prevailing market price for a massive amount of stock. Instead of buying a hundred shares at ten, you get to a million shares at ten.

LEMAN: If you have a totally dark business, the trades still have to print at a printing facility. The question is, will there be more transparency in future? The ability to understand where that trade printed is built into the technology. It is just not disclosed by the printing facility. Regulators must access it when they conduct a market investigation. If some stock takes off like crazy, it will no longer be the New York Stock Exchange or NASDAQ trying to investigate if there was insider trading.

Where does the regulator go to find out that information? How many places do you have to look to see that a particular person, or a particular series of people, took advantage of the market and covered their tracks by being in different liquidity pools? You will have to find a way to take that information and do a reconstruction of the activity. That may lead to more transparency about which of these dark pools' marketing information is actually equal to what they are really printing in the market, to what they are really achieving with their liquidity. That is not publicly available currently.

MCCOOEY: NASD, a regulator, now runs the TRF, the Trade Reporting Facility. NASD has access to that TRF information.[7]

SMALL [From the Floor]: But it is not at market.

MCCOOEY: True. I agree that it cuts both ways. But there are certain groups that want to know what is traded, and there are others that obviously do not want that information displayed. That is the friction in the market.

BONI: I have an observation. I do not know if you are familiar with the way self-help[8] works in a Reg NMS world. Let me explain. If I am trying to get to Arca and I cannot get there for some reason, first I have to assume that it is down. The SEC people can clarify this. Then I can declare self-help. At that point I can trade-through them. We are just not clear whether they were really down, or whether I have a problem. It has been fascinating to figure out how we will deal with that situation as brokers. What are our policies and procedures to make sure that we are doing all we can to ensure that the problem is not on our end?

It is interesting just watching, for example, the number of times the New York Stock Exchange declared self-help against Arca, or Arca against NASDAQ. This will be one of the ways in which people can start seeing these venues sorting themselves out. I would not be surprised if there is an outfit that is already figuring out how to publish these kinds of statistics. Maybe the academics in the room will start to provide information to the public. I would also be curious about whether an academic group will take a look at whether or not we see more trades-throughs or less.

One of the quirks about the Reg NMS trade-protection rule is that protection is at the top of the book only. But having found that, the venue can rip through and trade-through any of those quotes that are inferior to the top. We may see more of those retail liquid orders being traded through because they were not at the top of the book at the time.

HOLOWCZAK: Thank you panel very much. And thank you audience for your questions.

---

[7]The TRF was established in November 2005 to provide OTC trade reporting for transactions executed internally in all NYSE, NASDAQ and Amex-listed stocks.

[8]Under Reg NMS, a broker was permitted to "trade through" the best price whenever that price was unavailable to complete the execution of the order under terms acceptable to the customer. In these instances, where there is no public price that permits the broker to complete the order, it can engage a "self-help" strategy. As originally envisaged, the broker could internalize the order, or execute the order against other orders on the broker's books. Also, regulators instituted "self-help" for instances when a market is experiencing a system's breakdown. For example, say an investor is unable to access the best displayed quote on a stock at the New York Stock Exchange because of technology problems at the exchange, that customer could declare self-help, bypass the exchange and execute his trade on another exchange.

Chapter 3
Dialog with Erik Sirri

Erik Sirri and Bob Pisani

ROBERT SCHWARTZ: Welcome to this session with Erik Sirri and Bob Pisani. Like all the other great sessions here today, I am looking forward to this next one with much anticipation. I have known Erik and Bob for a long time. Erik and I have co-authored a Harvard Business School case together. In the process, I learned a lot from Erik about writing a convincing business school case. And, of course, you are all familiar with Bob Pisani of CNBC.

BOB PISANI: Thank you Bob. Most of you know Erik as Director of Market Regulation at the US Securities and Exchange Commission. Holly Stark and I were just talking about him a few nights ago. The SEC broke with tradition when it hired Erik, who is an academic. Traditionally, the head of market regulation is a lawyer. Maybe Erik, a distinguished economist, brings a different perspective to the SEC. In any event, the industry speaks highly of Erik, as I discovered when I called around to ask what I should discuss with him. The procedure here is simple. I will talk with Erik for about 25 min. Then I will invite questions from the audience. Erik said he is willing to discuss just about anything. Nothing is off the agenda.

Let's talk a little about the news, Deutsche Boerse's bid for the ISE.[1] I know you cannot talk about the bid itself, but this goes to the heart of the globalization of stock exchanges. Can you talk a bit about how the SEC views this in the context of global, around-the-clock, 24-h exchange trading? I do not mean in terms of exchanges buying each other.

Let me ask you a very specific question that has always bugged me. Why is the London Stock Exchange trading screen not available here in the United States? Is there anything, practically speaking, that would prevent this? Would the SEC object?

E. Sirri (✉)
US Securities and Exchange Commission, New York, USA

[1]In April 2007, Germany's Deutsche Boerse announced it was acquiring the US-based International Securities Exchange (ISE), the second largest equity options exchange in the US, for $2.8 billion. The acquisition was completed on December 20, 2007.

R.A. Schwartz et al. (eds.), *Technology and Regulation: How Are They Driving Our Markets?*, Zicklin School of Business Financial Markets Series,
DOI 10.1007/978-1-4419-0480-5_3, © Springer Science+Business Media, LLC 2009

ERIK SIRRI: Before I answer, I have to offer my standard declaimer that anything I say represents my own opinions, not the opinions of any of my colleagues, nor any of the commissioners.

Why are London screens, along with trading in the same shares that occurs on these screens, not allowed here? The most straightforward reason is because London is not a registered exchange in the US. For exchanges to come here and trade their securities, they must be registered. London could have registered here anytime. But it is not a practical proposition. So the question you are really asking is this: Why would we stop an exchange from putting its electronic screens – and trading its shares – on desks in the US?

We are having a conversation about this at the commission.[2] That said, maybe it is time to reconsider our position. The basic reason is the reality of how shares are traded today. Think about an institutional investor. Institutional investors have access to foreign shares. That is a good thing. Otherwise we would not have diversified portfolios. So whether they are, mutual funds or any other funds, professional institutional investors have been buying foreign shares for many years. They have done this by developing correspondent relationships with foreign exchanges, either through a foreign broker, or through one of their correspondent brokers.

On the retail side, if you are a particularly active trader, you can access foreign shares through various types of electronic brokers. That screen is not sitting on your desk in the US, but a US broker is facilitating access to those shares. So, at the SEC we are asking, if you put in prohibitions, what are the practical benefits? There are costs because of them. And it seems the intended benefits are not really there.[3] Accordingly, we are asking ourselves difficult questions about how we can get foreign screens to come into this country.

If we allow the foreign screens here, what protections must we put in place that are consistent with the core mission of the SEC – investor protection? There are questions of law; for example, what jurisdiction does the transaction happen in? There are the practical questions. For instance, what if these foreign exchanges retain different books and records? What if they do not have a suitable auditor? What if something happens in the area of market manipulation that requires us to track down an order at the exchange? Our chairman feels strongly about finding a

---

[2] The conversation in question was about the concept of "selective mutual recognition." Specifically, as broadly envisaged in discussions, pending approval of this concept, certain non-US financial services, such as the London Stock Exchange, would not have to first register in the US to provide services here to local investors. These foreign intermediaries could then, for example, operate their trading screens in the US provided they were "supervised in a foreign jurisdiction under a securities regulatory regime substantially comparable (but not necessarily identical) to that in the United States," as the Securities and Exchange Commission noted in a release dated May 24, 2007.

[3] Sirri is referring to the current costs associated with executing trades in foreign markets for US investors. These investors can, for example, buy and sell foreign securities through a US broker that has a correspondent arrangement with another broker-dealer, such as an affiliate that trades outside the US on a foreign exchange. However, indirect costs could accrue from higher commissions, currency fluctuations, time zones and operational charges, compared with potentially lower costs if the foreign shares were traded "directly" here in the US.

solution. Last week a group from the SEC was in Europe talking to various exchanges. This was a topic of great interest.

PISANI: Do you mean that you are reconsidering whether or not these overseas exchanges need to be registered in the US, or, are you saying that there may be some other way to allow them into the US to trade here?

SIRRI: We do not have the answer to that yet. However, we will probably host a roundtable later this year[4] and invite people to offer their opinions. You can imagine electronic traders, sell-side professionals, all sorts of folks attending. But yes, we are trying to step away from a too narrow reading of our regulatory principles, which, of course, are designed to protect the investor but could have a potential downside if they are too narrowly focused. Is it necessary to have registered foreign exchanges with registered shares, if these overseas stock exchanges wish to trade in the US? Are those protections always necessary? For example, if a foreign exchange operated here in the US markets, we might allow the foreign shares to trade on it – but perhaps not allow some US domestic shares to trade.

The idea is that US investors would know that when they trade on the New York Stock Exchange, NASDAQ or another US exchange, they would be buying registered shares on a registered exchange with all the attendant protection. But if you step over to the London Stock Exchange or the Paris Bourse – these would be unregistered shares. They would be registered in their home country but not registered here. And you would be playing by the rules of the game in the jurisdiction of that foreign exchange.

PISANI: Let's talk more about competition between exchanges and the type of consolidation that we are seeing. How is this viewed at the SEC and what concerns, if any, do you have about this global consolidation?

SIRRI: We do not have a dog in this fight, per se. We are regulators who worry about market quality and investor protection. It is business forces that cause exchanges to consolidate. So we can talk about consolidation, or at least about a business combination that is done. For example, the New York Stock Exchange and Euronext have formed NYSE Euronext. That was a holding company transaction. There is a top-level holding company in place, Euronext is over there, and the New York Stock Exchange sits over here. Early on they will look for technology gains. After that, it is hard to tell. John Thain will be here today, so you should ask him. There is no point in me answering for him.

In my personal opinion, technology is the first area that is looked at in a merger of this kind. It is hard not to imagine that at some point they will want to combine those liquidity pools. But I do not know. There are regulatory challenges and business challenges before that.

---

[4] The Securities and Exchange Commission hosted a roundtable on mutual recognition in June 2007. "The roundtable explored whether selective mutual recognition would benefit US investors by providing greater cross-border access to foreign investment opportunities while preserving investor protection," the agency announced. In early 2008, the agency put on hold a plan to develop a proposal for mutual recognition because of the departure of two commissioners.

PISANI: Do you have any concerns in general about the move towards global consolidation?

SIRRI: No. I do not think so. Look, from our perspective, the businesses will do what they want for their own reasons. There are benefits that will come with global combinations. As an example, you will get better products from the exchanges. Distribution will be more efficient. It should be cheaper to reach those shares, or reach those contracts when they occur in the United States. I do not think that the SEC has a particular concern in these areas.

Now, if they happen in the US, where we use a central regulator, we would be concerned that adequate protections are in place. For example, if a foreign entity buys a US exchange, what we care about is that the folks at that exchange – at the top of that holding company's structure – show us their books and records and audit trails. It is important that the core SRO functions of a US exchange are not impaired by new ownership structures.

PISANI: Let's talk about the competition for liquidity at the NYSE and elsewhere. There is a lot of talk about a decrease in NYSE market share – the internalization of order flow, and routing to other liquidity providers. Average trade size has dropped with advances in algorithmic trading. There is the rise of large liquidity providers such as, for example, Liquidnet. There are non-displayed markets, or dark pools of liquidity. Do we need more disclosure of dark pools of liquidity? What concerns does the SEC have about this?

SIRRI: I am not sure that we have any concerns right now. We want to understand how markets are working. You asked about competition. There is competition for orders. We have a somewhat different model than most other countries. We really have let a thousand flowers bloom. You heard people say earlier that there are about 40 places, market venues, where you can buy a particular name. That is a very, very different approach than other national regulators take. Now, with this comes some issues, such as connectivity and linkages that provide solutions to market fragmentation. I agree with Ian Domowitz, who spoke earlier – you do not hear the word fragmentation used as much any more. The reason is that the electronic market linkages are pretty efficient. So we have good competition for order flow. And that was part of the reason for Reg NMS.

On dark pools, I have read a lot of stories, which said that something wrong is happening in these dark pools and that the SEC is looking into them. I think about ATSs and dark pools in a very structured way. I would say that we do not have concerns about them per se. We are watching and trying to understand them. We are trying to know what their market share is. We also want to understand why and how people use them. To me the phrases "ATS" or "dark pools" are a little bit like the phrase "hedge fund." These are very broad terms that cover a multiplicity of purposes and styles, to the point where they do not help us to understand what is happening. We do care about issues with ATSs. For example, ATSs are dark pools in the sense that they are opaque; that they are not producing information about quotes. So, you can see why we would care about someone leaking information on them.

Access rules for ATSs are different. An exchange, by and large, must take all comers. But ATSs, because of small volume, do not have to take all comers. They can, at some level, discriminate between who comes into their systems. That is not necessarily bad. You can structure an ATS to appeal to a particular kind of trader; for example, a passive trader. They could offer a certain kind of passive pricing, and an active trader would not want that. This may, in fact, facilitate the ATS's business model and consequently, they discriminate on that basis. We will not care about that as long as that ATS does not get too much of the volume. As that ATS's volume grows, then that ATS starts to become more important as a market center.

Then there are rules within Reg ATS, which say that you must become more and more transparent. As you think about the world today, you do not just have a few central exchanges. You have 30–40 or so venues. That makes the choice about best execution for a broker far more complex. I am not sure that is an issue that has been completely thought through. Best execution obligations today – post-NMS and post-30 or more ATSs – are more subtle and more nuanced than they were previously. Trading professionals should be thinking about this. So, for example, you could not today just route to the New York Stock Exchange to satisfy your best execution obligation. Why? Because at the New York Stock Exchange their router will protect their top of book. That is terrific, that is compliant with Reg NMS. But it would not protect below the top of the book. There is no obligation for them to do so.

You can see where a broker would have an obligation to treat their customer's orders fairly. Now, when you have someone routing other order types, you can ask them the question, how should they think about the ATSs? Did they have to go to every single ATS every single time with an order? No. That is not realistic. Can they never go to any ATS ever, and justify that? That could raise some issues.

PISANI: You mentioned best execution. Can you give us an update on Reg NMS?

SIRRI: March was the latest phase of Reg NMS. There is another phase coming up in late summer. Folks were a little concerned before that last phase started rolling out, but it went pretty well. Leslie Boni mentioned the "self-help" question earlier this morning. We have monitored self-help, and we are keeping a record of self-help. We signal very directly to the firms that when NMS rolls out its phases, do not feel shy about declaring self-help. We do not want the market to break down. We want the process to be smooth. A number of firms have availed themselves of that, and that is terrific.

Going forward, we have heard the complaints. People call in, but we want to be sure we understand why self-help is being declared. Is everything declared perfectly at all times? No. But we would care about a pattern of self-help that is abusive for certain purposes. You do not have to be too creative to think about why someone might do that. So, we are paying attention but we do not see any big concerns.[5]

---

[5]One of the concerns is that broker-dealers and other players, seeking to competitively disadvantage an exchange or another market by declaring "self-help," would regularly bypass them for stock executions at inferior prices on others markets. For example, a player could seek to reduce market share in securities traded by, say the NYSE, by frequently abusing the self-help provision to send orders to another market.

PISANI: Let's talk about the role of intermediaries. Let's talk about specialists and market makers. I work on the floor of the New York Stock Exchange. Are intermediaries an endangered species?

SIRRI: That is a good question. Let me explain what industry professionals are telling us. Essentially, they are saying that their business proposition is not what it used to be. It used to be that they sat at the center of a market, as some type of a market maker, and that they had certain advantages. They had better access to the order flow compared with other market participants. These market makers may have had informational advantages. Whatever you call them, they were structural advantages.

On the other hand, they may have had a set of obligations as well, obligations about fair and orderly markets, about handling orders, etc. There was an implicit balance between the advantages and the obligations. Today, as you start to see the 90%-plus of orders in previously manual markets handled electronically, these intermediaries are saying that folks off the floor are too smart and too fast. They are coming to them with orders too quickly. Frankly, as a business proposition, being on the floor is a lot less interesting than sitting off the floor, playing by their own rules instead of the specialists' rules. This should not be a big shock any more because the world has changed.

Industry folks are now asking for changes in the set of obligations and benefits that market makers have. The changes asked for relate to their ability to discriminate amongst different types of traders. These changes may have to do with things like their stabilization rules or price improvement obligations, but as a general rule they are looking for change. As a regulator, we do not have any interest in picking one business model over another. We do not want to decide whether a market should or should not have market makers because we could not guess the right answer. It is not an appropriate concern for us.

What we do care about is the quality of the markets. We are more interested in the outcomes than in the input. When people come to us with a proposed change they must make the case to us that it works, that it should improve the quality of the markets.

PISANI: Is there any sense from the SEC that intermediaries need some kind of relief? That their obligations now outweigh the benefits of trading?

SIRRI: We are having that conversation with industry professionals. We are putting it up to them to propose the changes that they would like to see, and to be prepared to justify their proposals on the basis of market quality.

PISANI: Turning to listings on US exchanges, I have another question. Now that it is a little easier to de-list in the US markets, a number of companies who had ADRs and ADSs – American Depositary Receipts and American Depositary Shares – here have announced that they are going to de-list. British Airways did it. The media statement from them was that we have volume that is fairly low. Frankly, compared to the volume that we are trading in our primary markets, the regulatory and accounting costs do not make it justifiable. Does the SEC have any role in promoting some kind of global regulatory or accounting standards? Some way to make it easier for these companies to list here as well? They seem to be making some kind of statement, in addition to low volume, about what it costs to maintain two separate books. Did the SEC have any role to play here?

SIRRI: In a way, the question you are asking is a different side of the same coin about foreign markets coming to the US. We posted a rule recently that says that, provided that your trading volume is sufficiently low, you as a foreign private issuer can de-list off the exchange. What you are asking about is international financial reporting. If you are a foreign private issuer trading here, you must reconcile your foreign accounting rules with US GAAP, or Generally Accepted Accounting Principles rules. That is costly. We think that it does not provide a lot of benefit to most investors. So, we have proposed eliminating that reconciliation. That came up last week.

More to the point, we have discussed the possibility of a Concept Release[6] that would give US issuers the option of either reporting under US GAAP, or IFRS, International Financial Reporting Standards. And that would be a sea change. We are not saying that this is immediate. It is a number of years down the road. But this would be saying that we would not hold out reconciling foreign and US GAPP rules as the one and only way to list in the US. Certainly, foreign issuers could be held to a more global set of accounting standards. That is a big change. It is part of our acknowledgement of how global these capital markets have become.

PISANI: It is time for questions. Yes, sir?

FRANK HATHEWAY (The Nasdaq OMX Group) [From the Floor]: The SEC seems quite pleased that the Reg SHO[7] pilot study showed what we all kind of knew, that the price test for short-selling in penny trading does not make any sense any more. We are now in the rollout phase for Reg NMS. We now have the access rule in place. We have best execution obligations. Can we use these few months, as well as the first phase of the roll out, as a pilot study to see if the full compliance obligations for the order protection rule are necessary? Or, can we get to where we need to be with what we have in place today?

SIRRI: You mean an informal kind of pilot? In other words, can we analyze what we understand? The answer is, if you want to collect information and present it to us, we will be happy to look at it. But if you mean a pilot in the sense that, based on the outcome of the pilot, we would go back and change our view of the order protection obligations that would probably be pretty unlikely.

PISANI: Yes, sir.

ROBERT WOOD (University of Memphis) [From the Floor]: In most countries, equities and derivatives have a common regulator. Suppose that, as a trader, I am going to trade on my screen, say in Canada, where a product can be regulated by a

---

[6] Concept Release on Allowing U.S. Issuers to Prepare Financial Statements In Accordance With International Financial Reporting Standards (Corrected) (Release Nos. 33-8831; 34-56217; IC-27924; File No. S7-20-07; August 7, 2007).
[7] SHO, enacted on January 3, 2005, introduced new standards for short selling.

common regulator. Given the separate roles of the CFTC and the SEC, that same product might have difficulty getting implemented here in an efficient manner. Is there a concern about that? What are the barriers to preventing a combination of these two agencies? Perhaps a big one is the Senate agriculture committee, controlling the futures. That perhaps is the big source of funding for them. So what can be done?

PISANI: When will the SEC be more like the CFTC (laughter)?

SIRRI: Let me answer Bob's question first. The point you raise is valid in that, outside the US, most regulators are unified in the sense that derivatives, banking, insurance, and securities come under one umbrella. That is obviously not the case here. The introduction of screen-based trading in the United States can pose particular product based issues for us. For example, one regulator may say that this is a terrific product, another may say that it is problematic for us. Even the jurisdictional questions can be difficult. We are w orking with the CFTC on various kinds of products to make this easier, even for domestic products.

The point you raised is that the problem is elevated when those products are foreign. I agree. We will have to find a proactive solution to this problem. How we do so is anyone's guess. Congress has a lot to do with keeping these things separate. That does not mean that we at the SEC cannot work constructively with the CFTC. In fact, we are working together now on credit derivatives. We are working with them to try to get products to the exchange markets, whether they are, for example, security-based swaps or future products.

As to your more general point, we are conscious that, if an SRO of an exchange wants to change their rules in the US, generally there is a Notice and Comment process. Sometimes you can do it more rapidly but, still, there is generally a Notice and Comment process. A lot of exchanges operating locally do not have the equivalent of that. Rule changes can happen much more quickly. In some cases exchanges do not even file rule changes with the local regulatory agency. That puts pressure on us as trading screens come here from overseas and trading becomes more global.

It will be very difficult as the central regulator in the United States to competitively disadvantage our exchanges because we have a different process for approving rules. At the same time, we have a core investor protection mandate. How do you balance that mandate with the competitive pressures coming from these other exchanges? The answer is, we do not know. We are having that conversation at the SEC. It will take cooperation among the regulators, and it may take help from the Congress.

PISANI: We have time for one or two more questions.

GRANT VINGOE (Arnold & Porter LLP) [From the Floor]: You mentioned the foreign screen discussions. One of the other ideas being floated is access for foreign brokers and institutional investors. It is presented as if the issues involved are the same for brokers as for the exchanges. I am wondering if they really are equivalent in your mind, or whether it is possible to separate the concerns of brokers and exchanges. The exchange issue obviously implicates all of the disclosure obligations for issuers, but institutional access by brokers seems a lot different.

SIRRI: By and large they can be separated. There are no Section 12 disclosure requirements for issuers. Here's the framework: A foreign broker cannot walk into the

United States, because it would be unregistered. Their customers could be institutional or retail, except, under a certain set of circumstances, which are governed by rule 15a-6.[8] We are giving some thought to rolling portions of that back, and we are asking, what protections are really necessary when a foreign broker deals with a US investor? If the investor is an institution, then perhaps we can roll some of those protections back, including the chaperoning requirement of 15a-6.[9] We are looking to free up that interaction a little bit, thus cutting out some of the cost in the process.

On the retail side, we have to catch our breath because in the United States the broker is a gatekeeper in various sorts of ways for retail investors. It is true for institutions as well, but especially for retail investors. We place obligations on brokers, and it is easy to imagine how a foreign broker would not take them seriously. The protections for retail investors, the suitability requirements, the safeguarding of funds, all these things would be very different in a foreign regime. In a nutshell, we will move in that area. I can see the SEC doing it for institutions far more than for retail investors. There is the question about where you draw the line for what an institution is.

PISANI: One more question?

STEPHEN SAX (FBN Securities Inc.) [From the Floor]: Hedge funds are relatively strong, with a trillion dollars in assets. They contribute tremendous volume on all the different venues. And they are unregulated. I see how much money some of these hedge funds are making. Even the small ones make significant amounts of money. Is anybody looking to see that these hedge fund transactions are played by the rules and regulations of the SEC?

SIRRI: As you probably know, there was an SEC rule on the registration of hedge fund advisors that was overturned in the Second Circuit. Hedge funds bring up three types of issues with a regulator. The first is effective protection issues. The second is market quality issues, including manipulation, and insider trading. The third issue is systemic risk. On investor protection, the SEC took a run at that with registering the advisors; the court said no, and that was the answer. With respect to market manipulation/market quality issues, federal securities laws apply, so hedge funds, even though they are not registered – the advisor is not registered and the fund is not registered – they still cannot legally manipulate the market, cannot engage in insider trading, and the anti-fraud laws apply.

The third, systemic risk, is where most of the attention is focused. The President's Working Group, comprising the Treasury Secretary and the Chairmen of the Federal Reserve, the SEC and the CFTC, talk about these issues. A couple of months ago, we issued a set of principles called the Principles for Private Pools of Capital. In some sense these were aspirational principles. They were not quite best practices. They asked about the things that folks in the process should be doing. What should they be paying attention to? What kind of information should they get?

---

[8] Securities Exchange Act of 1934.

[9] The rule permits unregistered foreign broker-dealers to conduct business in the US provided they are "chaperoned" by a US broker, which, technically means, for instance, that certain business of the foreign broker in the US must be done only with the US broker physically represented.

The President's Working Group, by and large, took the view that market discipline was probably the best thing that was called for. That said, we pay particular attention to issues with risk, including systemic risk and counterparty risk. There is a trilateral group of the Financial Services Authority in the UK, the SEC, and the New York Fed dealing specifically with issues about credit derivatives, equity derivatives, and the lack of sound record keeping, the novation of the contracts. Things were not settling out well. So we have been spending time on those issues. At the same time, we have been trying to get a hold of the systemic implications. But there are limits to what we can do.

PISANI: Our next panel will move right into regulatory initiatives. Erik, thank you very much (applause).

Chapter 4
Regulatory Initiatives: Implications for Competition and Efficiency

Frank Hatheway, Leonard Amoruso, Douglas Atkin, Daniel Gray,
Richard Ketchum, Douglas Shulman, and Robert Wood

ROBERT SCHWARTZ: I interact regularly with Frank Hatheway. Over the years, Frank has been most helpful to me. Moreover, we share something in common: Both of us are professors. On that note, it is a pleasure to have you with us here today, Frank.

FRANK HATHEWAY: Thank you very much, Bob. Let's start with a question for the panel. As Erik Sirri of the SEC noted earlier today, investor protection is the big enchilada for the regulators. For the most part, efficiency and competition are secondary objectives for them. Indeed, efficiency and competition have to co-exist with the regulatory obligations of the brokers and exchanges. In addition, you have the technological changes and the associated costs that were discussed this morning. So, from your organizations' perspectives, and from your own perspective as experts in this field, my question is this: Is regulation driving competition and efficiency? Or is the process more reactive? Is competition actually making us more efficient? Is competition driving us to achieve certain things that will then alter the regulatory landscape? Len....

LEONARD AMORUSO: Since my two primary regulators are sitting on my left, I will include my own disclaimer that these are my views and not those of my firm. And if you do not like what I say they are not my views either (laughter)!

Looking back over the last couple of years, even the last few decades, you will discover that most regulation is reactive. At its core, regulation is typically designed to address some of the views or practices that we are seeking to change. However, in recent years, we have had regulation – or at least a portion of it – that is proactive, that is a driving force for change. For example, the move to decimalization a few years ago was a proactive force for change. It was not really designed to address a specific abuse, trading practice, or behavior. Rather, decimalization was designed to modernize the markets by replacing fractional increments with trades priced in decimal amounts, such as 5 cents, similar to the increments of most commodities and other products that trade in the US markets.

F. Hatheway (✉)
The Nasdaq OMX Group, New York, USA

R.A. Schwartz et al. (eds.), *Technology and Regulation: How Are They Driving Our Markets?*, Zicklin School of Business Financial Markets Series, DOI 10.1007/978-1-4419-0480-5_4, © Springer Science+Business Media, LLC 2009

The consequences of decimalization can, of course, be endlessly debated, but I am sure we agree that the result is tighter spreads, better technology, more competition, and more overall benefit to the consumer. While it may be difficult to quantify in terms of price, we can agree that efficiency has improved dramatically since decimalization.

Regulation is also a reactive force for change, designed to address a specific behavior. An example of this is the perceived abuse of short selling, or extended fails. Many would argue that perhaps Reg SHO was not the best approach.[1] Nevertheless, if you compare the NASDAQ threshold list[2] that existed back in 2005, it did have an affect on the market. A recent letter from the NASD to the SEC stated that in 2005 there were 148 securities that had extended fails of at least 77 days. Fast forward to April of this year: there were less than 12 securities on a similar list, so did it work? Was it necessary? Did the end justify the means? Perhaps.

One piece of rule-making that was reactive ultimately led to the NYSE hybrid system. There are components of the hybrid that came about in response to perceived trading abuses. On the proactive side, it would spur more transparency and more liquidity. It is a little early to tell the outcome, but this rule making has both proactive and reactive elements.

DOUGLAS ATKIN: To borrow a phrase, the SEC does a great job of shedding daylight on magic, and in promoting transparency. For example, the agency introduced the order handling rules and made the NASDAQ trading markets much more efficient for investors. Limit orders were protected, which required market makers to publicly display more price-quote information. The SEC later introduced decimal pricing, which created more opportunities for investors.

At the same time, the regulators have cast the spotlight on specialists, and the subsequent investigations have also been beneficial for investors. Indeed, we have read various stories from both the buy-side's and sell-side's perspective in the *Wall Street Journal*, and in other media, about the continuing attempts to reform the NYSE floor.

The latest issue to hit the press is questionable practices between hedge funds and large broker-dealers. Generally speaking, I would say that nothing egregious is happening. Nevertheless, we are shedding daylight on questionable practices, whether they are related to proprietary positions at the big houses, or in the trading rooms across Wall Street. So I have to say, the SEC has a great record of bringing matters like these to light.

---

[1] Reg SHO, enacted on January 3, 2005, was aimed mainly at stopping the abuse of naked short selling through new "locate" and "close-out" standards. The locate requirement meant that a broker needed a reasonable belief that the equity to be shorted could be borrowed and delivered to a short seller on a specific date before the short sale could occur. The close-out standards were the increased delivery requirements for securities that had many extended delivery failures at a clearing agency.

[2] Threshold securities were defined by the Securities and Exchange Commission for the purposes of Reg SHO as equities that had an aggregate fail to deliver position for five consecutive settlement days at a clearing agency, totaling 10,000 shares or more, and equal to at least 0.5% of the issuer's total shares outstanding.

DANIEL GRAY: I am required to tell you that my opinions are my own. The question is whether regulation is generally proactive or reactive. The obvious answer – and the correct answer maybe 90% of the time – is that regulation is reactive, but with little twists. Once the regulation is in place, inertia sets in. New regulation can cost some people money. It typically takes something like a crisis, or outdated regulation to prompt a regulatory change. In this case, you get a little twist, which may explain what Len was talking about. Once the political will is there to address the root cause, it prompts something to be done. Inside the agency, but elsewhere also, people try to step back. They are reluctant to just tinker with an existing problem. They attempt to bring some foresight. You try to be proactive once it is clear that something needs to be done.

RICHARD KETCHUM: I agree with everything that was said. That just shows how times have changed. I do not remember a time when we agreed on everything on many panels in the past.

Constructive regulation is more proactive than reactive. It is hard to think about any market structure change in the last 25 years without concluding that the SEC has significantly impacted those changes in a positive, pro-competitive way. The approach by the agency has been beneficial and fundamentally proactive.

At a self-regulatory organization like the New York Stock Exchange, market structure often requires reactive changes. SEC regulation often demands a rapid response from the SROs. Indeed, the NYSE's reaction to the SEC's adoption of Reg NMS will, 6 months from now, significantly impact the roles of specialists as they interface with orders, primarily electronically-delivered orders. They will have less access to color in the market, and market information in general, as a result of dramatically increased electronic trades. That will, in turn, lead to changes in the Exchange's regulatory game.

You will continue to see adjustments and tweaks in regulatory requirements in response to a very competitive environment. Because of the different role specialists play today, we are making changes with respect to their stabilization requirements;[3] how we look at the specialist's negative obligations[4] and, finally, at what a real specialist's risks are compared to an earlier period in which order flow was more substantially controlled which resulted in lower capital requirements.[5] We can expect to talk more with the SEC about rule requirements built into the NYSE hybrid system.

---

[3] At issue were changes in the how much of their own capital NYSE specialists were required to use to reduce and handle volatility during trading to stabilize the markets.

[4] Negative obligations are the requirement to match buyers and sellers directly without "interpositioning" when a match can be made at, or within the quote. For example, if there is a buyer and seller available on a stock trade at the same price quote, the specialists has a "negative" obligation to match that directly.

[5] It is important to note that by mid-2008, the NYSE proposed rules that would abolish the traditional function of specialist, or designated market makers (DMMs), as they would be renamed. DMMs would reportedly retain their role as primary liquidity providers and be permitted to trade other securities, such as derivatives. However, one crucial change is that the new style specialists would no longer have a first look at electronic orders before they are publicly displayed.

There are also questions regarding existing restrictions on trading by specialists that are unique when compared with restrictions on any other market participant. The restrictions simply may not reflect the realities of today's competitive market environment. You can expect more conversation on this subject with the SEC in the coming months.

From the standpoint of upstairs trading, it is an important time for rethinking models. For example, the logic of having rules that are quite unique for the NYSE is becoming less compelling in an electronic world where competition is greater. So that leads us to question things like NYSE Rules 97 or 92, and whether to harmonize those requirements with NASD's Manning Rule.[6]

Furthermore, there are also questions about how floor brokers and specialists interact with markets away from the New York Stock Exchange, and whether they should be able to do that directly from the floor. These changes require pushing against decades of thinking at the New York Stock Exchange, which once viewed itself as an island. At a time like this, regulation has to respond to how markets have changed. At other times, being proactive made a great deal of sense. That is how the SEC operated in the last decade.

DOUGLAS SHULMAN: Like Rick, I also agree with my fellow panelists. In some ways this notion of regulation vs. competition sets up a false dichotomy. Yet, regulation works very well if is done right by participants on both sides. The basic premise of regulation is a fair deal for investors so that they will participate in the capital markets. As a result, there will be capital formation, and the people who are regulated will be able to make money and engage in competition.

Are regulators proactive or reactive? We are spending a lot of time understanding where the market is going, and we are studying the demographics. Regulators, like businesses, have to allocate resources, which are limited. I will give you a couple of examples that certainly are proactive in protecting investors. We looked at the trend of the retiring baby boomers and the related statistics. We could see, for example, that in 20 years there will be 73% more retired people than there are today. Consequently, we started studying trends like packaged products and new products in development. There are a lot of them and that innovation is great.

Take a look at some of the initiatives that we have undertaken recently. We had a *Notice to Members* last year that talked about best practices in product rollouts. This was not a rule. These were no enforcement cases. These were best practices in cooperation with the industry. We talked about a proper suitability analysis to make sure that the right customers for the products are being targeted, that sales training was suitable, and that adequate monitoring was done.

You will see the regulatory and self-regulatory communities working cooperatively with the industry to achieve results more often. In the end, it is not about having a

---

[6]For example, the Manning Rule for NMS stocks and over-the-counter securities, and NYSE's Rule 92 for listed securities, both governed the handling of customers' limit orders with separate disclosure and compliance obligations. Ketchum has publicly advocated a single regulatory approach.

rule for everything, but about trying to figure out where the market is moving; where the industry is trying to head, so that we can take advantage of that. What can we do together to make sure that there are no problems on the front-end, so that we do not have enforcement on the back end?

We had a well-publicized issue with mutual fund breakpoints in which mutual fund customers were not getting the appropriate benefit. We have had some enforcement in cases of egregious conduct.[7] We also used the regulatory bully pulpit to bring together the mutual fund producers and brokerage distributors. We set up a Task Force, and talked about the issue. Two things came out of that. One was aimed at harmonizing the rules and terms so that, for instance, you have a common definition about rights of accumulation. Second, we worked with the mutual fund industry to create a central database that the brokerage industry could access to find information on mutual fund breakpoints populated by the industry.[8] Again, we did this as proactive regulation.

I think that you will see the regulatory community and the brokerage community working together to harness technology on disclosure. We had a two-page Internet-based disclosure document at the point of sale for mutual funds. SEC Chairman Cox has been vocal about mutual fund disclosure. The industry is trying to figure out the best way to deliver the right information to customers before they make a purchase or sale. It is in everybody's best interest to get it right, to harness technology and the Internet to get better, clearer disclosure to customers. Customers should be protected on the front-end, so that you do not ultimately have to resort to heavy-handed regulation on the back end.

ROBERT WOOD: I agree with Rick and Doug that effective regulation need not stifle competition. A brilliant example of proactive regulation is that which compelled the adoption of the penny tick size because it resulted in a huge reduction in trading costs. Penny ticks, in conjunction with changes implemented under Reg NMS, has resulted in much greater competition for listed order flow as reflected in the decrease in NYSE equity market share.

HATHEWAY: All right, ladies and gentleman, you have an opportunity for questions.

HAROLD BRADLEY (Ewing Marion Kauffman Foundation) [From the Floor]: My question for both the regulators and the users of the capital markets goes back to what Erik was asked in the previous session. Are we sitting on a time bomb with

---

[7]Mutual fund "breakpoints" are discounts to customers who buy funds with sales charges, or "loads." Breakpoints are, in effect, volume discounts based on the size of the investments. The SEC and NASD have had enforcement and disciplinary action in this area. In early 2004, they announced actions against 15 firms for failure to provide breakpoint discounts during 2001 and 2002.

[8]The Task Force report on mutual fund breakpoints, published in July 2003, recommended a central database that has breakpoint information for all funds that have front-end sales charges. The NASD worked with the National Securities Clearing Corp. (NSCC) to create this database and the NASD urged the fund industry to "populate" the database with information on each fund's breakpoint discounts. The report had a total 13 recommendations, including a more standard use of typical account terms, such as "minor child."

derivatives now representing four times local GDP?[9] Investors are unable even to understand how much paper has been issued against equity and bond transactions in fundamental risk transactions and private paper over-the-counter derivatives. To me, having lived through the late 1980s, when Joseph Jett[10] reportedly put tickets in drawers, we are now at the level where Wall Street is generating immense revenues with other people's money. I am hearing that regulators, even in private transactions, are trying to say let us not undermine public confidence in the markets. These products are working well for now. But is this issue concerning derivatives not the next regulatory crises?

HATHEWAY: Let's start with the industry people.

AMORUSO: Risk monitoring and risk assessment is a growing and critical part of our business, whether it is how we interact with our clients, use our capital, or manage our own portfolios. It is an absolutely vital component to the operations of any dealer. It certainly is something we pay very close attention to.

ATKIN: I agree with Harold when he said that investors are unable even to understand how much paper has been issued against equity and bond transactions in fundamental risk transactions, and private paper over-the-counter derivatives. He asked are we sitting on a time bomb, noting that derivatives now represent four times local GDP. I do agree that this represents a very significant risk. The market has dealt with smaller systemic risks and blowups in the past, but this risk which he has identified would be a dandy. I am not sure if the regulatory response should be proactive or reactive, but I will say that the brokerage firms have just done a masterful job. In some ways, these fancy derivative products are part and parcel of their business model. It is in the dealers' self-interest to market them to investors, so I would simply say, *caveat emptor* (buyer beware). You can argue that is up to the buyer to be conscious of the risks. However, I am not sure that everyone needs these products from a risk perspective.

HATHEWAY: Before the regulators answer the question, let me add that, obviously, as an issue comes before you, you have supplicants who are interested parties. You have to weigh all these things up. Doug is the one smiling the most. Dan is doing a good job with a straight face. So Doug, why don't you take this one first?

SHULMAN: I am smiling because we do not believe that we deal with supplicants (laughter). Let me lead my fellow regulators by saying that there is no way that I

---

[9] Bradley's question turned out to be prescient. Later in 2007, the global credit crisis that erupted was blamed on the massive size and complexity of derivative products. For instance, research firm Celent estimated the collateralized debt obligations, or CDO global market at $2 trillion in late 2006. CDOs are a kind of asset-backed security and structured credit product.

[10] Joseph Jett, a government bond trader at Kidder, Peabody & Co., was accused of perpetrating major trading fraud in the early 1990s with US Treasury bond strips. After it was discovered, his employer reversed over $300 million in trading profits that Jett had reputedly booked. In 2004, the Securities and Exchange Commission ordered Jett to forfeit $8.2 million in bonuses, fined him $200,000 and barred him from any association with financial trading.

am going to step deeper into this (laughter). Erik Sirri alluded to one of the primary jobs of regulators in this fast-changing market – it is cooperation and deep dialogue with participants in the market who are innovating, and with other regulators. The question that Harold raised is kind of, as Erik said, like throwing out the phrase "hedge fund."[11] It means a lot of different things to a lot of different people. Most of the regulators will be very focused on making sure that where there is a gap in the market on issues like jurisdiction – either in the US or across borders – that there is dialogue and cooperation among the regulators.

HATHEWAY: Richard?

KETCHUM: Let me give you a double disclaimer that these are my own personal views and do not reflect either the New York Stock Exchange, or the NYSE's SRO. Harold, your point is clearly valid. There is good news and bad news. Those of us who have lived through market structure changes recognize a certain history here with respect to non-transparent markets and the variety of successful unbundling efforts by the industry. The combination of non-transparency and unbundling at different times has resulted in blowups.[12] Financial firms often trust their model while ignoring that no model effectively predicts market movements on the tail end.[13] Liquidity reputedly predicted by models in times of stress has been consistently proven wrong over generations, if not centuries, as far as our ability to really understand liquidity demands and securities. All of those are good reasons why you are right to be concerned, Harold.

You probably raised the greatest regulatory challenge facing us today. Let me speak from my experience working for Citigroup, and the things we have seen firms implement. First, from the standpoint of intermediaries, there is no longer the gap with respect to looking at holding companies that existed in the past. There have, however, been improvements. The SEC's consolidated supervision program has filled in those gaps with respect to non-bank financial firms.[14] The level of global cooperation on a regulatory level between banking and non-banking organizations today allows for a more sophisticated analysis of how those firms process risk, and of how they manage conflicts across regulated and non-regulated entities.

Second, once again, speaking only for the intermediaries, changes made by the SEC have transferred a variety of capital risk positions from the intermediaries to

---

[11] See, Sirri, Chap. 3: "To me the phrases 'ATS' or 'dark pools' are a little bit like the phrase 'hedge fund.' These are very broad terms that cover a multiplicity of purposes and styles, to the point where they do not help us to understand what is happening."

[12] At issue is the fact that some firms, such as hedge funds, are loosely regulated, while others are much more transparent. It has inevitably led to market blow-ups, the speaker argues.

[13] A classic example is Long-Term Capital Management, a US hedge fund that developed complex models aimed at making profit from fixed income arbitrage. Despite the model, the fund failed in the late 1990s, which led to a bailout by major banks and investment houses.

[14] The SEC supervises securities firms on a group-wide basis under its consolidated supervised entity (CSE) program. In other words, the agency oversees not only the US-registered broker-dealer, but also the consolidated entity, which may include foreign-registered broker dealers, banks, and the holding company. The CSE program, has, in effect, filled in the "gaps" that had existed.

the regulated entities that are, at least, regularly reviewed and examined by the SEC and NYSE Regulation. This was truly a critical step. It has resulted in a dramatic repatriation of risk and hedged positions to the regulated broker-dealer. Another thing that is happening right now is portfolio margining. It deals with the fact that the present options derivative margin treatment have moved many hedge fund positions away from the regulated entity altogether.[15]

The third area of concern is the tremendous concentrated risk in non-transparent hedge fund positions by the prime brokerage units of major broker-dealers.[16] The President's Working Group on Principles and Guidelines on Private Pools of Capital is pretty thoughtful on this issue. Those of you who view it as basically an abdication from a regulatory standpoint need to read it a lot more closely. In fact, pieces of it would scare the hell out of me if I were still sitting in a broker-dealer firm. One fascinating paragraph talks about the obligation from the standpoint of broker-dealer prime broker intermediaries to monitor the *overall* leverage risk of a hedge fund customer. That is opposed to just the leverage they choose to show you from a prime broker standpoint. It is not clear how that will be done. But I take comfort in the fact that the regulators are grappling with that responsibility.

HATHEWAY: Dan?

GRAY: I have to let discretion be the better part of valor here. My boss just responded to that question at the last session. He said that it was being handled at the President's Working Group. So I will just reiterate what Erik said (laughter).

WOOD: We want regulators to maintain trust in our markets. Our financial markets are built upon trust. Any action that undermines trust – that is, investor confidence –harms the markets. Many recent examples of actions that undermine trust come to mind – Enron and Arthur Anderson in the business world, and market timing and front running in the trading world.

What do we want from our regulators? Regulation should foster competition similar to what resulted from penny ticks and Reg NMS, as noted earlier. On the other hand, Sarbanes-Oxley was a regulatory overreaction to scandals that led many international firms to list in London rather than in the US. Another example of overreaction was the SEC's response to shredding, which resulted from the rents generated from excessive Consolidated Tape Association fees. The SEC required trading venues to write regulations to stop this shredding, rather than take a more appropriate approach – dealing directly with the fact that the arcane CTA organization is incapable of restructuring their fees to eliminate the rationale for shredding.[17]

---

[15] See, http://www.nyse.com/pdfs/PortfolioMargin_101707.pdf

[16] At issue, is the lack of substantial data to regulators about the size of hedge fund risk and positions.

[17] Tape shredding occurs when a trading participant breaks up a large transaction, say 250,000 shares, and reports it as 2,500 trades at 100 shares each, to, in effect, inflate market data revenues. In rules aimed at stopping the practice, the SEC stated: "No member or associated person may engage in conduct that has the intent or effect of splitting any order into multiple smaller orders for execution... for the primary purpose of maximizing a monetary or an in-kind amount to be received...."

AMORUSO: What do we want from our regulators? That is an excellent question. That really is the subject of a tremendous amount of debate. It was the subject of Secretary Paulson's recent summit between business leaders and government leaders, where he posed the question of whether or not we have struck the right balance between investor protection and market competitiveness. We want to make sure that we not only have a sound and trustworthy system, but that we also have a system that gives companies the flexibility to compete and to respond to changes in the global economy.

In addition, the US Chamber of Commerce issued its report earlier this year where it deals squarely with that issue. The report actually argued that we need to take a fresh look at regulation. The Chamber supported a much more cooperative environment with our regulators. It also argued that we need to employ cost–benefit analyses when we go forward with new regulation and have an open dialogue with industry participants, so that the government will indeed get the benefits of experience and expertise in formulating best industry practices. As an industry participant, we obviously are very supportive of those types of initiatives. We have a long way to go in the US to make sure that we have a more cooperative relationship between business and regulators, and that we must conduct these cost–benefit analyses.

There are a lot rules that are reactive in nature. Dan Gray indicated that about 90% of them are reactive in nature. We must look at the cost – history has shown that the ends do not always justify the means. The means are a significant cost in this industry and to the consumer as well. So, we will pay close attention to them.

HATHEWAY: Doug? What do we want from our regulators?

ATKIN: The regulators have done a pretty good job of pointing out, on a macro level, what they would like to see, whether it is increased transparency, or companies talking to more people before they release information to the general marketplace. There has been a successful record of the market adjusting to these kinds of regulations from a business point of view. However, the regulators have an extremely mixed record of tinkering with micro market structure. For example, the SEC, in my opinion, has legislated market fragmentation. You can call it competition, but the markets inexorably go towards one dominant liquidity pool. In free markets around the world, whether it is Deutsche Boerse, the Hong Kong Stock Exchange, or London Stock Exchange, the vast majority of all trading occurs in one place. So it artificially keeps fragmentation in the market. It is counter-intuitive, but it raised costs for investors. However, I don't have a dog in the fight anymore, that is for sure.

HATHEWAY: Dan?

GRAY: The easiest part, which I am sure people always seem to get wrong anyway, is trying to estimate the out-of-pocket cost of compliance. The more difficult part is how do you estimate the benefits of a regulation? Or, on the flipside, how do you estimate the cost of not regulating? How do you estimate the cost of a future very bad event that might happen because you did not regulate now? Obviously it is very hard to gather objective data. There are lots of assumptions. There are lots of opinions and theories. You try your best because it is extremely important. You do not want to get it wrong.

Doug is absolutely correct. A key element of the US regulatory regime, particularly the market structure regulatory regime since Section 11A was added to the Exchange Act in 1975, is competition among multiple markets trading the same stocks. The statute that required competition also created this fragmentation. The last 30 years have seen this exercise in balancing competition and fragmentation.

We want competition. We want the positive things that competition brings – better pricing in trade execution, innovative technology, and those sorts of thing. But competition can create fragmentation so we do things to address the fragmentation, whether they are successful or not. That balancing is at the core of the regulatory regime for the last 30 years. That explains what I think Erik alluded to earlier: why in the US we do have a lot of competition, and the foreign markets do not have a lot of competition. Unlike the foreign markets that do not have a lot of competition, in the US markets there are several key elements to the way we promote competition and minimize fragmentation.

First, transparency. In the US markets, everybody gets to see everybody else's prices. Second, there is non-discriminatory access to markets. A lot of what we do at the Commission when we assess exchange rules is this. We ask ourselves if the exchanges are trying to exclude people from a market. Are they trying to reward the people that they like, or push other people out of the market? Another element is non-discriminatory clearance and settlement of a transaction, so that no matter where you do a trade you will be able to have efficient clearance and settlement. Another really important issue is, how do you go about evaluating the cost of having lots of competing markets? We are now up to about 60 markets if you count exchanges and alternative trading systems. What is the cost of price impact for the large investors who are trying to trade in size if we do not have as much liquidity as we would have in a market that is consolidated?

HATHEWAY: Rick, you have done a lot of thinking on different types of regulatory philosophies?

KETCHUM: There are two types of situations that I believe a proper regulatory philosophy must address. In instances of foreseeable failures where investors were harmed, zero tolerance is understandable and appropriate. As we have experienced industry compliance failures and more complex markets, one of the primary areas of focus for regulators everywhere over the last decade has been to encourage firms to adopt more effective compliance controls. In the last few years, regulators have focused on senior management and on raising the stakes for them in the compliance area.[18] That, along with private litigation, has largely encouraged the industry to commit far more resources to compliance. It is a beginning. But it is not a fully balanced regulatory environment. It leaves a level of distrust and problems in communication, as Len referred to. That is the challenge that we and the NASD have been wrestling with for the last few years.

---

[18] Ketchum's office identified the Sarbanes-Oxley Act of 2002 as an example of how regulators raised the stakes.

In the future we need to increase the level of industry-regulator dialogue, and look to provide a level of flexibility, for the industry to make risk-based control decisions. We must deal with situations where there is a failure of control, in the sense that investors were not actually injured, but where the risk of injury to investors was increased by the firm's negligence. On the other hand, we may also have situations where a firm has demonstrated that commitment to compliance and appropriate senior management accountability, and where a rule violation was episodic without direct harm to its clients. In those situations, we can take the enforcement route less often.

SHULMAN: I agree with Rick that the dialogue between the regulator and the firms is very much in focus. The answer to your question about what we want from the regulators can be found across the industry, and from all our conversations about what suitable regulation will look like in the next 10 years. How is it evolving?

A good example is a merger between the New York Stock Exchange member regulation and the NASD in the creation of this new SRO.[19] This is an evolution that will enable us to move forward in a sensible way.

We recently had a mini-dialogue with the firms, which Rick was more involved with than I, about the gifts and gratuities rule.[20] Some firms preferred that it be principle based. They said, we are adults; we will watch and make sure our people are doing the right thing. Other firms said, just tell us how much we can spend on a dinner (laughter). This has been an ongoing dialogue that will get a lot more air.

Finally, rather than trying to define all the benefits and costs ahead of time, we are running a look back. The first look back we are doing is OATS, the Order Audit Trail System rules.[21] We are asking, what was the intent when the OATS rules came into being? How have the rules played out? What benefit have they given to investors? Are they working as intended and should we change anything? We really have no promises of what will come out the back end. There are lots of moving pieces in changing regulations that have become part of the fabric of the market. But at least we are committed to making the look backs and running these analyses.

HATHEWAY: James?

ANGEL (James Angel, Georgetown University) [From the Floor]: Bob Wood, you raised the issue of market data. I would like to hear the opinions of all of the panelists

---

[19] FINRA, or Financial Industry Regulatory Authority, is the name of the new organization that was formed from the consolidation of the regulatory functions of NYSE and NASD.

[20] In 2006, the NASD issued *Notice to Members 06–69* to look at weaknesses in how firms handle Rule NASD 3060. This rule prohibits any member, or person associated with a member, from giving or sanctioning the giving of, a gift item in excess of $100 per individual per year, when the payment is connected to the business of the recipient's employers.

[21] OATS allowed the NASD to recreate events in the life cycle of an investor's orders and more completely monitor the trading practices of brokerage firms. Most importantly, OATS required that all events of a trade to be recorded with an accurate time stamp.

about what kind of market data you think we should have. As many of you know, in the 1970s there was a de facto nationalization of the market data from the exchanges, and the creation of an almost Stalinist collective for the dissemination of the data.[22] Technology has changed a lot since then. Regulations have changed a little. What kind of market data regime should our public policy work for?

HATHEWAY: Len. I keep hitting on Len, but you pay the bills!

AMORUSO: It is interesting to discuss what is happening in New York right now with market data. Who actually owns the data, and who can you sell it to? As a generator of a large amount of market data, both in terms of trades and quotes, we would certainly like to see a move towards a regime that rewards those who generate the data and that rebates as much as possible back to the firms that are generating it. It is interesting now at a time where you have this dynamic between quotes and trades as to how the split will actually be looked at.[23] I think that certain exchanges right now are grappling with how they will quantify that. Some Exchanges are paying market data rebates back based on trades, and some Exchanges are also paying market data rebates for your quotes. But we would like to see a continued move toward the reduction of cost where you can do so. We would also like to see those firms that are generating significant portions of the data being rewarded.

HATHEWAY: We have reached the end of this thoughtful session. I would like you all to join me in thanking the panel (applause).

---

[22] Beginning in the late 1970s, SEC-registered exchanges and market centers trading NYSE and AMEX-listed securities have sent their trades and quotes to a central consolidator. That is where the Consolidated Tape System (CTS) and Consolidated Quotation System (CQS) data streams have been produced and distributed, in a process overseen by the Consolidated Tape Association (CTA).

[23] See STA Special Report – US Market Structure 2008: 'The pricing of market data may be the most controversial dispute. The Net Coalition and other non-exchange market participants believe that the data fees must be related to the cost of producing this data, and the SEC's Concept Release on market data suggests that a cost-based standard should be used in the case of fees charged by a "monopolistic provider"…The rebating of market data fees has also impacted market structure as business models have been created to take advantage of opportunities created by this competition. The SEC has recognized the significant impact of market data fees, saying, "Some SROs rebate substantial market data revenues to the market participants that contribute to creating the market data…."'

Chapter 5
What the Buy-Side Needs

Joseph Gawronski, Paul Davis, Fred Federspiel, Robert Gauvain, Oscar Onyema, and Daniel Shaffer

JOSEPH GAWRONSKI: I am pleased to introduce our next panel: Paul Davis, a passionate follower of market structure who recently retired from TIAA-CREF, where he is still active part-time; Fred Federspiel of Pipeline Trading; Bob Gauvain, director of trading at Pioneer Investments; Oscar Onyema of the American Stock Exchange; and, finally, Dan Shaffer, who is the head trader and owner of Shaffer Asset Management. (Paul and Fred, incidentally, are both PhDs, in mathematics and in experimental nuclear physics, respectively.)

I will start with a very popular topic: dark pools. What should traders do to access all meaningful pools of liquidity – pools that have decent amounts of liquidity – within the rules and regulations as markets continue to fragment? Does success depend on having all the appropriate tools on your desk, as well as using brokers and exchanges routing orders?

PAUL DAVIS: New tools are required in the hands of brokers, or in the hands of the buy-side. This latter side of the industry is evolving. For example, consider the various execution management systems, or EMSs,[1] that are being sold to the buy-side. These EMSs have been on the market for some time. Now, they are trying to reach into the dark pools. The brokers are hiring people who are looking at how to reach all the liquidity providers.

ROBERT GAUVAIN: When you look at how to access the dark pools, you must be prepared to work with brokers and some of the EMS platforms, and have them work with you to accommodate your needs. You have to ask them where they reach, how they achieve this, and how they can help you. The broker neutral platforms – platforms such as Pipeline that are not affiliated with any particular broker – tend to be more willing to work with you to come up with ideas and solutions to help you find the

---

J. Gawronski (✉)
Rosenblatt Securities Inc., New York, USA

[1]An EMS, or Execution Management System, electronically facilitates the application of trading strategies and the routing of orders to exchanges and other venues for execution. EMSs can standalone from an OMS, or Order Management Systems, which are used to manage and keep track of orders. With the advent of more advanced electronically trading along with the introduction of direct access to exchanges, EMSs became increasingly popular. EMS providers include Portware and Flextrade.

R.A. Schwartz et al. (eds.), *Technology and Regulation: How Are They Driving Our Markets?*, Zicklin School of Business Financial Markets Series,
DOI 10.1007/978-1-4419-0480-5_5, © Springer Science+Business Media, LLC 2009

different sources of liquidity.[2] It is a hand-in-hand relationship. In the ideal world, you should be able to access different sources of liquidity in a relatively easy way, but that is not the case. With a broker consortium, such as BATS or BIDS,[3] you find volume in them, but it is essentially a second look at that liquidity. The members of that particular consortium have already exposed it to their internal dark pools before they release it to the consortium. If you get a hit, and find stock in the consortium, you sometimes need to find a way to circumvent that platform and find the original source of liquidity. That has been our experience. For example, you may have found a small amount of liquidity in BIDS offered by a broker in the consortium – and then, after the transaction, you are still looking for more liquidity. You know who the brokers are in the consortium but you do not know who offered the liquidity because BIDS, after all, is an anonymous system. So, you may randomly try the individual proprietary algorithmic platforms of the various consortium brokers, in the hope of finding the broker who offered this liquidity, picking a strategy within that platform that taps into this broker's internal dark pool only. This way, it doesn't search outside of the broker's internal system. It is a hit-and-miss process, and you are literally searching in the "dark." That is one strategy to find more liquidity.

GAWRONSKI: Dan, you use algorithms in your portfolio management trading techniques. How do you hit all the liquidity pools?

DANIEL SHAFFER: We are a buy-side firm managing money in commodities, currencies and equities. On the equity side, we test the waters. By testing, I mean we aim for certain levels of pricing – such as certain lows and highs – based on algorithmic numbers, or electronic programs we have designed. In this approach, we want to buy at a certain high price, for example, because we know there is a seller there. We aim to find the liquidity in the markets. Usually the prices we trade at are in round numbers and century numbers – priced at over 100 – or at new highs or new lows. In our case, you will find a lot of liquidity at these price levels. If we are a buyer or a seller in a huge amount of stock, we will post a market order and see who shows up. Then, all of a sudden, sellers will come out of the woodwork and start showing themselves when they see an aggressive buyer. Our system shows us buyers and sellers, and depth in the market, and who is bidding and asking at the same time on my order. Our platform includes NASDAQ Level 111 data and NYSE data. If I want to buy 10,000 shares, and I know that up 50 cents I can potentially get those 10,000 shares executed, I will put in a limit up 50 cents, and I will buy all the offers all the way up. Usually the number of shares on the other side is very small. Consequently, when I indicate or show a large chunk of stock, everybody

---

[2] The different sources of liquidity here would, for example, include Pipeline and Liquidnet.

[3] BATS, which stands for Better Alternative Trading System, was established as an ATS in Kansas City, and it was later granted exchange status by the Securities and Exchange System. BIDS Trading operates the BIDS Alternative Trading System, a joint venture of investment banks that include Bank of America, Cit, Credit Suisse Group, Merrill Lynch and Goldman Sachs.

typically shows up on the system with the contra side interest. That is one of the techniques we use to find liquidity in these dark pools.

GAWRONSKI: Let me move to fragmentation. Is it getting out of control? Erik Sirri from the SEC said earlier at this conference that the SEC looking at dark pools. The SEC does not seem to be particularly concerned, nor is there is any action threatened, or a suggestion that the agency is going to change the requirements for dark pools. But there is a lingering feeling, as it looks right now at dark pools, that the SEC will step in at some point. Some participants feel the agency could do this because of the growing significance of dark pools, and the potential implications for market structure down the road. Do they need to? Are we near the point where so much liquidity in the dark is decreasing order interaction? Oscar?

OSCAR ONYEMA: From my perspective, fragmentation is an issue. I believe algorithmic aggregation is the way to address it. When that fails, the SEC needs to take a look again at the Fair Access rule of Reg ATS[4] from an aggregate perspective. If you are doing an inordinate amount of trading in the dark and, at the same time, you are relying on prices that are set in the transparent markets, there has to be some kind of test. In this instance, that test has been amended under Reg NMS from 20 to 5% of the average daily volume, on a security-by-security basis, on each individual dark pool and ECN. However, this misses the aggregate perspective. For example, if you have 20 dark pools each executing close to 4% in one security, the combined volume on the 20 dark pools could amount to almost 80% of the overall volume in the security. That is a significant amount of volume. Yet, you are relying on 20% of the volume in this security – displayed in the transparent markets to all participants – to set the prices for the 80% traded in the dark pools. There is a dislocation here.

GAWRONSKI: Fred, how do you see it at Pipeline?

FRED FEDERSPIEL: We think it is very good for market structure to facilitate as much trading inside the spread as possible. So, having a significant percentage of trades go off inside the spread is not a bad approach. As long as the block trading facilities are strongly aligned with the retail market, the process works well. In the past, there were block-trading facilities like the Arizona Stock Exchange[5] that were not strongly linked to the retail price. Systems like OptiMark, which came on the scene in 1996, could arrange to trade at different prices from the pricing that was occurring in the NYSE, NASDAQ or Amex. Systems like OptiMark failed. The best approach, therefore, is aligning prices in the retail and institutional markets.

GAWRONSKI: Paul, I read a draft of the recent paper you wrote, exploring the interaction of retail orders in the buy-side market. I am curious about your perspective.

---

[4] Fair Access Rule of Reg ATS (Rule 242-301) was modified in connection with Regulation NMS to lower the fair access threshold from 20% of the average daily volume in a security to 5%.

[5] Led by Kidder-Peabody executive Steve Wunsch, the Arizona Stock Exchange, or AZX, was created in 1990 as an electronic call market for institutional customers. It received much credit for its advanced capabilities at the start, but it never generated sufficient volume to make it viable. AZX was finally shuttered in 2001.

DAVIS: Basically, my research[6] is attempting to understand how retail marketplaces and institutional marketplaces interact. I thought I might be able to model different kinds of markets, such as a normal retail marketplace along with a non-price discovery marketplace, a kind of a hybrid market. Then I would run simulations to get a sense of how these various markets would interact in an order-driven marketplace. The work is still in progress. My concern, based in part on the simulation work, is what happens when a lot of the retail order flow gets siphoned off. I am not as concerned about institutional order flow being siphoned off and traded elsewhere. That is because, quite frankly, the primary marketplaces are now constructed much more for retail-sized flow, whether it is actually a retail order, or an institution that is slicing and dicing its orders. My concern is that, if a lot of those thousand share orders are executed in dark books, where is the price discovery? I am coming down in the middle ground in this area. I am comfortable with dark pools for large order flow. We have been living with dark pools for a long time. When we called it upstairs trading in the past nobody seemed to worry too much about it. Institutions could get their orders done in those dark pools, or books. Now, it is an open question whether the Pipelines and the Liquidness are a better place to get those trades done today than the old upstairs marketplace.

FEDERSPIEL: Paul is right to worry about dark pools pulling orders away from the exchange – orders that could contribute meaningfully to price discovery, that is retail-sized orders that used to come to the exchange. As participants' access to the dark pools evolve, the dark pools can become a vehicle to step ahead of the best bid posted. That is because a midpoint-priced dark pool order is effectively priced at the bid, plus half of the bid-ask spread. Participants want to trade quietly, but ahead of other bidders. They do contribute to price discovery because their presence in the dark pool effectively replaces a trade that would have occurred at the bid with a higher-priced trade – one that gets printed at the midpoint. In general, these participants would be better off with an algorithm actively deciding the time to join in the dark pool. The randomness of an algorithm could help limit their contribution to the price discovery by confusing predators. I do share your concern about people blindly piling in, not really understanding exactly what it is they are contributing to price discovery.

GAWRONSKI: We wrote a piece a few months back with a Wizard of Oz reference entitled, *"Pricing, Product, and Speed, Oh My!"* which explored these three components of an exchange. With Reg NMS and technology, high speed has become a reality across the markets. Pricing to me seems very competitive. There is practically an announcement every other day about some price cuts, or increased rebates

---

[6] At the time of writing, Davis' independent research paper, "Comparing Market Structures: How Best Can Institutional and Retail Investors Co-Exist?" was still in progress. The author said he compared a conventional retail marketplace with a non-price discovery marketplace, running simulations of both. In an interview that took place after the conference, he explained he is seeking to ascertain the effectiveness of the latest US electronic market structure as he looked at retail and institutional order flow. He has concluded for now it is still an open question whether today's is the best type of market for institutional order flow.

from various execution venues for trades from market participants. But are we see-ing enough differentiation in the products in all these new electronic venues, and enough innovation to justify the market fragmentation?

As we heard on a previous panel, competition in the market is beneficial. A monopoly does not benefit anyone, even if you like the benefit of the centralized order flow. You have so many detrimental factors with a monopoly, such as a potential lack of innovation and higher pricing, that we need competition. But are we going a little too far? Is there enough new product out there? Are we going to see fragmentation that is not justified by gains?

GAUVAIN: As you work your way down, it is essentially the same offering with the different dark pools. In a similar fashion, is there any difference between the various algo platforms? It is almost like buying a car. You take the test drive. There are one or two things in the design you like that makes you want buy the car. Similarly, each of the dark pools has just one or two things that differentiate it from the others. Do you need all these features? Probably not. Is it good to have them? Absolutely.

I would much rather have something even if I did not need it. As for dark pool access, Paul is right. Trading in dark pools used to be called upstairs trading. As the market gets more and more fragmented, you must be able to find the sources of liquidity. Unfortunately, as the markets continue to fragment more, you will see more ways to get to those dark pools and to price discovery.

It is almost a Catch-22 situation. Nobody really wants to be trading based upon what they would consider retail market structure. On the other hand, no one wants to post a price, because no one wants to give up what it is that they are doing. Thirty-two years ago, on this day in 1975, the Securities and Exchange Commission mandated negotiated commissions for all securities transaction, finally abolishing fixed commissions. At that historic moment, the industry thought the trading busi-ness would end. But it survived and expanded – very well, as far as I can tell.

GAWRONSKI: Anyone else?

DAVIS: Since I retired, I have found that some institutional brokers have a very uncanny ability to reach into the different dark pools, and to find liquidity.[7] They end up doing a program at very low cost because of the liquidity that is out there. If you can find the broker who can reach out to all these different dark pools – or if you do it yourself – you have a leg up on the competition.

SHAFFER: We never wanted brokerage firms to have the ability to shop our orders, or know our positions. That, of course, would be revealing too much information. Dark pools and crossing networks have given us the ability to avoid this. We are now able to run an in-house program, an algorithmic program to access all the liquidity available upstairs that could not be accessed by our desk in the past. We are seeing our execution prices in line with out pricing strategies when we run an in-house program based on price and time and other measures. We feel we are accessing

---

[7] Among this group, David later provided as an example, platforms from Credit Suisse and from Goldman Sachs, which operates Sigma X.

this liquidity very safely compared to making calls around the Street. So, I agree with Paul, one of the positive changes from dark pools like Pipeline and NYFIX Millennium is that these systems don't have an ability to shop our orders because our positions, in effect, are not known by these brokerages.

FEDERSPIEL: Look at the *features* of these products: The retail-sized dark pools are copying the model that was innovated by Millennium. So I am not seeing differentiation and innovation. It might be that the product is the combination of features *plus flow*. If you have control of flow, then there is always the motivation to go to your dark pool, whether you have algorithm orders that are sitting in your dark pool, or you have retail flow. If you have to pay three-tenths of a cent to NASDAQ, for example, to lift the offer, you would really rather avoid that three-tenth fee and internalize it yourself.

GAWRONSKI: I want to talk about algorithms. Nighthawk, Dagger, Guerilla, Sumo, you name it. We have hundreds of names for these algorithms. There are 39 providers of algorithms listed on Bloomberg alone, each having five or six algorithms. We have an algorithm overload in addition to a dark pool overload. How does the trader pick and choose? Does transaction-cost analysis help? Are there any other tools that can help? Dan?

SHAFFER: Well, we do not use any of them. Actually, we have created our own in-house algorithm, which we use to locate those pools. A lot of the algorithms used by larger institutional investors are in-house algorithms. That is what I have found on my travels to conferences and in my speaking engagements, as well as talking with other managers who have more assets under management than my firm.

GAWRONSKI: People use algorithms because they have chosen to do this internally, so it must give you an edge. How do you manage the process? How do you perform the necessary analysis to make those algorithms work the way you want, and get the feedback you need?

SHAFFER: Our math is based on many years of experience watching market movements and studying order flow. This helps us as we try to set and modify our systems on a constant basis. We created the algorithms ourselves to make sure that we get executed at a decent, or acceptable price. We try to reach the dark pools and trigger the pools that will satisfy our order, using our own algorithms.

GAWRONSKI: Paul, you did some of your own development with algorithms at CREF. What was the process like? Did you experiment with other providers?

DAVIS: Back in the old days, there was nothing. We started developing algorithms in the late 1980s, when our focus was not on trading single orders – which participants back then were mostly thinking about – but on electronic basket, or program trading. Today, of course, most of the brokers have strategies for handling single orders – that is, slicing and dicing orders electronically – and basket trading is common. Algorithms are the only way to go in basket trading. In single order trading, I would much rather find a large block with a Pipeline, or a Liquidnet, and get it done in one fell swoop, rather than slicing and dicing it.

When we developed basket trading, it was really sort of by the seat of our pants. We came up with ideas, continued to develop them and to monitor trading performance. I have been asked what benchmark we used; and which benchmark I wanted to beat. I wanted to beat all of the benchmarks, and we did it pretty well. If you have enough data points, and if you are trading well, you will look good vs. a reasonable benchmark. On one day we might perform poorly measured by one benchmark, and do well measured by another benchmark. But as you aggregate enough days and data points – and if you trade well – you will show up well measured against any other benchmark.

At the very early stages, we started capturing real-time data. We monitored our trade vs. the real-time data not only at the end of each day, but also during the day. We were on top of all of the information in the marketplace on a real-time basis. And based on that, we continually made adjustments to our trading environment.

GAWRONSKI: Bob? Have you dealt with third-party algorithms?

GAUVAIN: Every algorithm is different. You have to know which one suits your needs. We have a protocol on how to go about doing things. First of all, we aim to find the natural buyer and seller using information we have at the desk. This information includes records of brokers' phone calls and indications of interest, or IOIs via Bloomberg, AutEx or NYFIX Millennium. When we get an order we try to find something, so we put a piece of it into a crossing network. We look to see how to start a trade. Our traders trade particular funds and how the stocks trade. They are expected to know which platforms to use. We bring vendors and brokers in on a regular basis to keep our traders updated about what the systems do, and any changes made to them. We do not have the technology to build it ourselves. We rely on the Street to do it for us.

GAWRONSKI: Fred, you recently made an announcement about entering the algorithmic space in a unique sort of way. Any comments that might be relevant?

FEDERSPIEL: Fundamentally, there are three different ways that people are trying to resolve the problem. First, brokers are offering a suite of different algorithmic styles. Second, firms like Electronic Specialists in New York are providing portals that you to a wide range of these pools. Thirdly, there is good progress on the application of TCA, or Transaction Cost Analysis, so there are now tools to help you choose which type of algos to use. We announced the Algorithm Switching Engine that will start later this month.[8] This program will allow you to select a style of algorithm that might perform well initially, and then will continually monitor market conditions to ascertain which type of algo would be subsequently most effective. The key here is to have that choice of different algorithmic approaches.

It is clear from some solid research that a certain type of algorithm can perform great under some conditions, horribly under other conditions. A simple example would be an algorithm that would try to get a buy accomplished by joining the best bid. That is terrific if the market is in a slightly volatile situation – every time you post a bid the market jiggles around and you are getting hit often. If the market is

---

[8] Pipeline's Algorithm Switching Engine actually launched in October 2007.

less volatile, it is not so terrific. You are not getting anything done, so you want to understand what types of market environment the algorithms work well in.

GAWRONSKI: Paul said he does not depend on algorithms when he has a block trade. It sounds like you are trying to allow someone to use an algorithm that does not mess you up on the block trade, if you use it intelligently?

FEDERSPIEL: The goal is to maximize your chances of getting a great fill in a block trading system, so you want to be very quiet in the way you are gaining access to all the retail-sized markets.

GAWRONSKI: Oscar, there seems to be increasing competition between exchanges and brokers, a topic that we touched upon today. Market data is one of those areas where there is competition. Also, brokers have announced their own dark pools. These broker consortiums look something like the exchange utilities. Exchanges are providing smarter routing because they have to under Reg NMS. NASDAQ announced more services for listed companies. It seems like there is a melding of the functionality provided by brokers and exchanges. Apart from that competition, there is also the issue of who needs the exchanges or the brokers. The brokers out there are shrinking, the exchanges are also shrinking. The buy-side participants can trade among themselves, maybe with help from venues like Pipeline. Oscar, please tell us about the competition between brokers and exchanges. Where do you see it going?

ONYEMA: The relationship between brokers and the exchanges is interesting because brokers are many things to the exchanges. They are customers; they are owners, they are also competitors, especially in the transaction business. We think the brokers have an advantage over the exchanges in their relationship with the buy-side, and they also have more flexibility than the exchanges with the dark pools. Exchanges have more experience than brokers with market data; exchanges are very effective and have expertise in distributing market data. So when you do compare them, the jury is still out. The brokers do not provide listing services; they do not provide a venue similar to an exchange where buyers and sellers can meet. On the other hand, exchanges do not provide some of the services offered by brokers, so the relationship between brokers and exchanges is very, very complicated.

SHAFFER: Regardless of the venue, it is a lot easier to trade a liquid than an illiquid stock. We will trade anything from a small-cap to an extremely large-cap stock, based on what our systems are telling us to trade. For example, consider a large order for a stock that is trading 5,000,000 shares a day. That is an easy order to fill because you really don't have to play with it. With a small-cap stock that maybe trades 300,000 shares a day, you have to get a feel for what will move that stock, for where the supply is, and where the bids are. Once in a while, we will call the floor on a listed stock to get a sense of how it is trading. We will not tell them our size, but we will get a sense of what the activity is, such as potential supply of shares from other participants, in the stock. That could give us an indication that somebody who has not shown his hand is on the other side of the stock.

On the over-the-counter electronic systems, when we are working on a stock that trades, for example, 300,000 shares a day, we look at the different levels of price that are on NASDAQ Level 111. For example, you have participants today flipping size, actually electronically putting in large amounts of shares, and then suddenly withdrawing this large volume. I do not know if you have seen this on your screens – a big size coming in mostly from hedge funds, and in black box strategies that are computerized – that all of a sudden disappears. Sometimes it happens because you have some trader out there "fishing" for opportunities. When you start trading the small-cap stocks it is almost like fishing. You got out to look for the catch. We will monitor the system for a small period of time, look at the bids and asks, and at the flashing of any sign that comes in below the market to see what comes in on top of us. When we put up a bid, sometimes someone comes in ahead of us and puts in another bid – and if they see we have size, they try to front run us. We see that a lot.

The prices are constantly moving in the large-cap names. In the smaller caps it is a little more of an art to try to capture the price you want. If you need to trade a lot of shares, your order can move the price one or two points. If you sit there and watch the screen, you can see other traders who actually do that – move the price. Then, all of a sudden, the sellers come in and bring it right back down again. We do not want the stock price moving. We want to get a sense for putting our bait out there, to see if there is a buyer or seller who is willing to take our side of the trade.

GAWRONSKI: On that note, listed markets have made dramatic changes over the past year or so. The Amex and the New York are adopting hybrid markets. How are the techniques changing on that side of the industry? For instance, how useful are floor brokers given that so many orders are now being handled electronically? Can you still get good fills using a floor broker?

There are, of course, limits to Direct Market Access, or the DMA[9] approach available through the New York Stock Exchange and Amex. The NYSE always had the DOT system.[10] Now the NYSE offers some functionality in the OTC market. But reserve and discretionary order types and features like that are limited to brokers and specialists. So, are the floor brokers more valuable, less valuable, or are they just being used differently?

SHAFFER: Years ago you could not trust a floor broker. We would make the phone call, provide the size, find out who is standing around, and what the broker could do. But the floor trader would throw some numbers out at us that were not as accurate as they could be. Today, in my opinion, these floor brokers are worried

---

[9] DMA, or Direct Market Access, is electronic trading that enables buy-side trading desks to bypass a sell-side trader and route orders "directly" to a stock exchange, or venues like ECNs, ATSs, or crossing networks. DMA is faster and typically cheaper than having the order handled by a sell-side trader, at least in the types of trading involved. (This type of trading is popular with high-speed oriented traders, and hedge funds engaged in algorithmic strategies.)

[10] DOT, or Designated Order Turnaround, was introduced by the NYSE in 1976, and it was later upgraded as a system known as SuperDOT for the direct electronic routing of relatively small institutional-sized customer orders to the exchange for execution.

about their careers. They are worried about their futures. So, they are being a bit more accurate, a bit more detailed, and a little bit more accommodating to my question, "What is it like there for size?" Today, I find that the floor is more accurate than it was a few years ago.

ONYEMA: From an Amex perspective most of our securities are almost like specialized securities. They do not trade as liquid securities do, and they need the specialists to step in to maintain continuity and depth in the market. And, as for your point about specialists being asked to do size, well the specialists do provide a huge service here, and the floor brokers do as well. The floor brokers are able to find the other side to do size, and to get price improvement. Today, they have reserve orders on the Amex. They are looking to make that available to everybody, including the people upstairs, and to allow people to also use those other types to do size. So when it comes to doing size, yes, you still need floor brokers. Yes, we see that they provide value. DMA – and automatic execution systems – mean that you don't really need floor brokers for the smaller size trades.

GAWRONSKI: Bob, you look like you are about to say something controversial!

GAUVAIN: I never had much value for traders on the floor except for a small handful of them. I have always lived under the adage, beware of specialists makings bids or offers, because traditionally specialists always had more trading information on stocks than the buy-side, and they rarely gave up information. They had an information and time advantage. As Dan said, floor brokers are fighting for their jobs right now. So these people are making an extra effort to keep business. However, any time you tell something to a broker on the floor, there is a potential for leakage.

GAWRONSKI: Eighteen months ago, when we were trading a big program upstairs if I gave a piece to our floor team, there were times we were getting more done in Pipeline than on the floor. That did not surprise me as much as the fact that we could not locate the contra-side on the floor at all. I mean, the other side of the trade was not even getting a look in the crowd. They were simply ignoring what was happening on the floor. Maybe they preferred other venues so much and worried about information leakage that they would not even bother to get a look. They were more comfortable in getting that block done in Pipeline.

In certain situations we ended up at the end of the day doing, maybe, 500,000 shares in Pipeline, and 400,000 on the floor. Fred, what are you seeing in terms of your order flow, and what are your customers saying? I am most curious about the last 6–12 months when there were big changes at the NYSE. There are reserve order types that people can use that are more hidden. Maybe that is an improvement on the way things are done on the floor?

FEDERSPIEL: Post-hybrid, the giant change on the macro level is that it seems more and more NYSE stocks trade like NASDAQ stocks. There is a wide range of users in the listed marketplace today. Bob noted that sending an order to the floor could have negative consequences including information leakage. On the other hand, you hear people say almost the opposite, that the specialists add value, especially in the new electronic environment.

DAVIS: I am a big fan of the New York Stock Exchange. There is still value added on the floor, but the New York has to be redesigned. In a computerized market, roughly 50% of trading happens away from the electronic-order driven market, according to data from Deutsche Boerse. Off-exchange trading is particularly apparent for large orders and other types of orders. I would just as soon see as much order flow as possible being transparent. I hope that the NYSE can make the necessary structural changes to maintain a vibrant price discovery in their marketplace.

HAROLD BRADLEY (Ewing Marion Kauffman Foundation) [From the Floor]: When Bob Schwartz started having these conferences years ago, we had fractional instead of decimal prices, and there were no dark pools. We had NASDAQ's SelectNet.[11] I have been both a trader and a portfolio manager. The portfolio managers looked for long-term returns and the trader looked for short-term returns. Today, when I look at the expected cost of a trade compared to when this all started, it is de minimis. A lot of us have talked about volatility. Was volatility, in part, enhanced by poor trading systems and poor interaction systems in the past; does the declining volatility now suggest we are at the end of the trading game? Is it time to start talking again about Bob Schwartz's long held dream of a call market to deliver an equilibrium-clearing price?

FEDERSPIEL: My view is that the only way a call can work well is if it is somehow coupled intelligently, or tied strongly to the continuous sub-block trading market. A very important piece of our approach, our design criteria, is to couple as much as possible with the traders' existing workflow. Traders are accustomed to continuous trading from 9:30 a.m. to 4:00 p.m. So, as we try to build liquidity in a block trading system, we are leery of taking on another challenge, so Pipeline was designed as a continuous system, rather than as a call market.

GAWRONSKI: For you guys with dark pools, the exchanges are your competitors today. What is the worst thing they could do to put you out of business?

ONYEMA: From an exchange perspective, we are coming up with our own version of dark pools. The Amex, for example, just got approval from the SEC to introduce the passive price improvement order type.[12] That will enable our various order flow providers to sweep our dark pool for possible price improvement, before they post or sweep the displayed liquidity market. Having been on the sidelines with dark pools we decided it would be better to provide our own product as a way to compete.

GAWRONSKI: There is a "if you can't beat 'em join 'em attitude" at the exchanges. Right now there is increasing use of the hidden order types by the exchanges and the ECNs. Traders have been using Pipeline, NYFIX Millennium and other systems for some time. But it seems that the ECNs and exchanges have started to come out

[11] NASDAQ's SelectNet electronically enabled traders to communicate orders to NASDAQ Market Makers and it also facilitated dissemination of order information to ECNs.
[12] Passive Price Improvement orders were approved as undisplayed orders that had to be inside the automated best bid and offer of the Amex by at least a tick, prior to execution. Specialists and registered traders could use these order types to offer price improvement electronically.

with these hidden order types that are not what one traditionally associates with an exchange. We are now seeing that line blur as well. I do not know if you guys have been using much of these new order types. But if you look at the statistics, they are being used quite a bit at the exchanges and ECNS.

DAVIS: Harold Bradley's question goes back to an earlier discussion that we had here on the relationship between brokers and the exchanges. Brokers can internalize lots of things that exchanges do, but the exchanges rely primarily on the brokers as their customers. If the exchanges would open up and go directly after the buy-side as their customer, they could do a lot in terms of changing the dynamics of the marketplace. It would be very interesting for an exchange to have a virtual pool, basically an electronic board, that institutions could trade on without using a broker to intermediate the order. It is something I suggested maybe 6 years ago. Exchanges have to change the business model.

ROBERT WOOD (University of Memphis) [From the Floor]: You were worried about leakage on the floor with large positions. Is that a similar concern with dark pools? There are some 40 of them. I have seen evidence that there can be leakage in the dark pools. Are you measuring that kind of thing? If you can publicly tell us about it, what are your findings?

GAUVAIN: There is leakage in anything you do in this business. We measure two of the dark pools. We have been satisfied with them. They are good. Do we get hurt once in a while? Yes, we do. Is it to the point where you are hurt by information on trading becoming public information? Someone mentioned earlier today that the dark pools advertise trades. That is a yes-and-no kind of scenario. Most of the time what is really happening is an electronic IOI, or Indication of Interest, from one dark pool to another, is basically saying, "Hey, I have some stock, can you use it?" Some dark pools are constantly searching and sending each other information – electronic IOIs – on the availability of stock. The customers using those dark pool platforms never see the IOI. In some other dark pools they advertise that they have been active in a particular name for a period of time; they may advertise during the trading day, or at the end of the day. They are trying to draw in more stock. There is definitely more leakage there; it is just a matter of what degree that leakage is at. You, as a customer, always want to remain under the radar, hoping that no one sees your footprints. However, it is not up to you as a customer to tell a broker how and what to do in their internal dark pool; you just need to know what happens in each different platform and use those venues wisely.

GAWRONSKI: Fred, when you announced you were excluding algorithmic providers, it seemed that had something to do with some type of – I don't want to call it leakage – but let's say confusion in your core community. I have seen TCA reports from you guys at times, but how are you looking at the leakage? How are you preventing gaming? How are you monitoring adverse selection? What is the feedback you get?

FEDERSPIEL: There are different approaches to dealing with leakage. If you take an institutional-sized order and post it in a dark pool, traders tell us anecdotally that after a few pings of that order have happened, the stock price can run away. What are the ways to deal with that? One very effective way to participate in that retail-sized market is to capture the valuable, uninformed retail component flowing through the dark pool. You want to confuse the predatory flow that sneaks into that mix. One way is with an algorithm that is deciding when we should be posted in a dark pool. We have a different approach. We work to segment off the predatory flow from non-predatory flow just bye setting a giant firm commitment for every stock, basically a giant, electronically executable order. This requirement, which could be 100,000 shares for a reasonable liquid stock, makes it prohibitively expensive for someone to troll. That is the approach that we have taken. There are many dark pools that take yet another approach: police the community and kick people out if they take advantage of the information that is systematically leaked.

GAUVAIN: How many people have you actually policed, or pulled out of the system, or suspended from use of this system? What are the number of suspensions?[13]

FEDERSPIEL: It is a small number, a handful. At Pipeline, instead of looking at the issue user by user, and simply eliminating users that took advantage of someone else in the community, a couple of times our response has been systematic modification of the system. We assume everyone, including you, would love to game other people on Pipeline, that everybody is looking to bring the maximum value out of any trading venue for their customer. So we make a change system-wide, because if one person has figured out a way to take advantage of the system, others could too.

As an example, one of the problems that we had was with our notification system, the Pipeline Block Board. When we first launched it, symbols would flicker too frequently, so that if people watched it closely, in certain cases they could discern if someone had a limit order. Consequently, we had to extend a random delay of the Block Board to eliminate this flickering – adding uncertainty to the calculations of anyone looking to game the system. .

SHAFFER: Any time you discuss or put an order on the platform, people know and talk about it. I trade currencies, which are now very much being traded electronically. I get e-mails during the day of where the size is, where the stops are. Once you have placed your order in the market, people know about it.

BROOKE ALLEN (Maple Securities) [From the Floor]: My answer to the question about what the exchanges can do is that they could be more aggressive in making sales calls on the buy-side. But here is my question. I am old enough to remember

---

[13] According to a 2007 buy-side survey by Tabb Group, 60% of the buy-side participants polled said concerns of gaming influenced their decisions on interacting with dark pools. In a later survey, released in August 2008 by Greenwich Associates, some institutional investors revealed a lack of knowledge on the extent of information sharing with other participants by dark pools, which are "dark" supposedly because trades are executed anonymously. Separately, one dark pool, Liquidnet, says it constantly monitored its system for abusive patterns of trading and gaming. A trader who is thought to be gaming is suspended from the system. Liquidnet has reportedly suspended about 100 members since it was founded some 7 years ago.

the days before the Internet. If you wanted to talk to a service bureau, you had to connect to their private network. Then, eventually, there were these sort of networks that could connect you. Today, there is just the Internet. It never even occurs to me what it costs to deliver an "electronic packet" from here to there. If all of this competition is supposed to be good for me, then why does sending a direct market access message cost me something, like, 5 cents a hundred, but I have to spend 10 or 20 times that amount of money to be able to go through some algorithm that unscrews up the marketplace for me? Why am I not seeing the benefit of this competition if there is supposed to be some? I should see that in my cost structure.

DAVIS: I think that you are seeing the benefit. Volatility is down. Trading costs are down, unless something happened in the last year or so. I think trading costs are down substantially.

ALLEN [From the Floor]: But they are not down relative to where it would be if there was just a central limit order book where I could send my messages. It is true that along the way in the evolution of the Internet, there were all these intermediaries that would take my packet and deliver it to a service bureau. But the Internet got rid of that. When you can go to Radio Shack and spend $600 for all the hardware you need to make the physical components of a central limit order book, it is not clear to me why I have to pay 10 or 20 times as much for all these algorithms that help me find where the other side of my trade is.

SCHAFFER: For the most part, we do not develop our own algorithms. We do in certain circumstances, but we generally use other people's algorithms because they are actually pretty darn expensive to develop and maintain. It is not as simple as just sending something from point A to point B.

ALLEN [From the Floor]: But a CLOB, if it is driven, is the answer

SCHAFFER: Right, but you know, we have Pipeline sitting here, and we have the AMEX sitting here. If we had a CLOB we would not have both of them. We would not have any competition.

FEDERSPIEL: Right, we don't have BATS sitting here. Is BATS the answer to your question? Is that the free CLOB that you have been wanting? It is making good progress towards reducing prices dramatically? There you have somebody who has taken an existing idea – the trading model of NASDAQ and of the ECNs – and replicated it in BATS. That is the thing that could be made almost free.

DAVIS: For a hundred-share order, it is a great way to go. But you might not want to put a million-share order into that Central Limit Order Book, because other parties are potentially going to use that information for their own advantage.

STEPHEN SAX (FBN Securities, Inc.) [From the Floor]: Paul, you mentioned that transaction costs are coming down. Are you talking about market impact costs, or just plain commission costs?

DAVIS: Market impact costs.

SAX [From the Floor]: Let us suppose you are comparing an actively managed fund with an index. Why is there such a performance difference between an active fund and an index fund? The majority of the active funds are not beating the index that they are adjusted to – on a risk-adjusted basis.

DAVIS: You have to take into account fees that the active funds charge. On average, the active funds probably outperform the benchmark, but not after fees. A recent study in the *Journal of Finance* got its arms around the persistence of good funds. The problem is finding the good funds. They exist, but it is hard for an individual to find them. Some outperforming funds persist, and so too do some under-performing funds.

FEDERSPIEL: In the recent cycle of the indexes, there have been a lot of under performers. But if you take into account the volatility in different time periods. There are a lot of really fabulous managers who outperform the indexes. They do not publish their performance. They are very private. The ones that are under-performing are the ones who advertise in the market and look for the retail order. But there are funds you have never heard of that perform very well.

GAWRONSKI: Larry?

LARRY TABB (The Tabb Group) [From the Floor]: Joe asked the question around Transaction Cost Analysis and algorithms. I do not think that anybody addressed it on the panel. You guys who measure the performance of different algorithms: Are there differences?

GAUVAIN: We do quarterly reports on broker's measurements. We also do algos and we break them out as a separate subset. We have a different code for each one of the algorithms, so that we can identify which system's network we used. We are learning which are the good ones, which are the bad ones as far as the actual numbers are concerned. Usually a trader knows whether it is a good trade, or a bad trade, when he walks out of the trading room. Now we have official measurement forms to judge a trading by.

GAWRONKSI: Let me relate a question about unbundling. Desks use brokers for a variety of reasons, including capital raising and research. In the early stage of algorithms, it seemed like the guys who were the most successful were the ones who were out marketing and building the algorithms first. Now it is getting to the point where people are really measuring these things. So, with respect to unbundling and the new clarification under those rules, CSAs[14] seem to have this new popularity.

---

[14]Gawronski is referring to the clarification of Section 28(e) of the 1934 Securities and Exchange Act, which sanctioned new Client Sharing Arrangements, or CSAs, in the US. CSAs are viewed as a strong step towards the complete unbundling, or the separating of research and stock execution commission payments. In the UK, a similar kind of unbundling measure, known as Commission Sharing Arrangements, occurred in 2006. Under traditional soft-dollar arrangements in the US, fund managers receive research and other services in exchange for sending stock orders to broker-dealers at higher than the lowest rates. CSAs permit a customer to instruct an executing broker to allocate a specific portion of commissions for research purchases from that broker, or from an outside research provider.

Personally, they do not seem that different from soft dollars. However, now it appears that people are more inclined to use them, at least when I visit clients. Over the next decade, let us say, how quickly will we see this unbundling happen? And what effects will unbundling have? Will we still use a certain algorithmic provider, or a certain broker, for a manual trade because of the research? How quickly will that change? How will that change the way the buy-side interacts with the sell-side and the exchanges, in terms of more direct use of exchanges? Will the buy-side look for brokers with the lowest commissions and overall transaction costs, rather than often having their choice dictated by the need to pay for the research?

ONYEMA: From our perspective, the exchanges do go directly to the buy-side. They do have direct access business. But it is difficult to compete when the brokers have soft-dollars arrangements with the buy-side. With unbundling, and with these newly popular CSAs, it might be possible to see a change.

GAUVAIN: We are in the process of finalizing a couple of CSA contracts, and we will be using CSAs soon. Over the last 3 years at Pioneer, we have had no real differentiation between soft dollars and proprietary research. In our view, anything above the cost of a pure execution is a soft-dollar item. When we structure our research, we set a budget. We work it out so that the portfolio managers and analysts are receiving a third-party service. That portion of the third-party service is deducted from their research vote, and then they work with that. As for CSAs, there are broker-dealers we value for research, but not necessarily for their ability to execute trades. They are the ones that we most likely pay through a CSA arrangement. Who could be a candidate for a CSA executing broker? A broker who has an excellent research product and trade execution skills; also a broker who does a great job executing trades but does not have a standing on our research list. Execution is everything! The brokers that we pay through a CSA arrangement will be invited to keep their lines open to us in order to trade, based on their flow of merchandise, but their research allocation will strictly be paid through a CSA arrangement. We also deduct what we consider the cost of execution from the total of their research vote, in order to come up with what we consider the true value of their research. The unintended consequences of CSAs, however, is that you may see some firms, predominantly the smaller and middle tier firms, taking a close look at their type of operation and say, "Geez, maybe trading is a cost that we do not need to incur given the amount that we are paid for our research, and purely research, and perhaps we need to address our entire business model." The growing popularity of CSAs will inevitably lead to consolidation among sell-side firms, and the elimination of trading desks as some brokers evolve more into research boutiques. It changes the whole evolution of the way that business has been conducted, as far as research and commissions are concerned.

GAWRONSKI: Fred, where is this going? I have found that if we are not pitching to a quant shop but we are pitching to a traditional shop that relies on research, we generally are only competing for only 10, 15, or 20% of their entire commission budget. Then we are usually thrown in the same bucket as the Pipelines and the Liquidnets, which makes it even more challenging. But you are in that same bucket as well oftentimes. Even if you can do things to facilitate soft-dollar payments, it seems that crossing networks have, in part, been capped by the fact that soft dollars, both third-party soft dollars and bundled commissions for bulge bracket proprietary research, are still the prevalent way of doing business in the equities world. How are you finding that? Is it limiting at all?

FEDERSPIEL: I agree that, in the past, there had been a natural cap in place at many firms. The commission dollars have been almost oversubscribed. They are owed to different parties who provide value research. The wonderful thing that happened since August was the terrific clarification of the 28(e) Safe Harbor provision. That has helped a lot.

GAUVAIN: As far as the changes in soft dollars and CSAs are concerned, let me say that we have been using Pipeline and Liquidnet as electronic trade execution platforms before the changes in soft dollars and CSAs took place. In theory, Pioneer has practices in place under the safe harbor provision that would allow us to have CSA arrangements with these two electronic platforms. However, we have pre-existing negotiated commission arrangements with Pipeline and Liquidnet, so I do not see us having CSA arrangements with them. I cannot justify raising my commission rates with two low-cost execution venues in order to have a CSA arrangement. Still, if Pipeline had just arrived on the scene today it might have been a different matter. For example, if they were charging 2.5 cents per share today, I might have negotiated that Pioneer get a penny credit for the CSA program, and Pipeline keeps 1.5 cents per share for execution. But since I am already being charged 2 cents per share by Pipeline I cannot justify marking up a commission on a low-cost execution provider, in order to get credit in a CSA arrangement. Pipeline and Liquidnet are in an entirely separate bucket as far as the new world of commissions is concerned.

WILLIAM HARTS[15] [From the Floor]: I have a question for the buy-side people on the panel. There have been comments in the press from maybe some mid-tier research providers about the fact that, maybe, they would not want to accept a check for payment for research. Do you see a time where you might have to cut off a firm with an analyst who you might particularly like because you do not want to trade with their desk, and they refuse to accept a check?

GAUVAIN: Would you rather have a 100% of something or a 100% of nothing? Most firms in this day and age would probably want to take a 100% of something. If that situation were to arise, I think I would like to pay them and be successful.

SHAFFER: No, we do not use another firm's research. We do our own research in-house.

GAWRONSKI: We will have to end on that note. Thank you, panel, for this excellent and thought-provoking session.

---

[15] At the time of the conference, Mr. Harts was Managing Director at Banc of America Securities.

Chapter 6
Market Quality, The Big Picture

Nic Stuchfield, James Angel, William Harts, David Krell, Andreas Preuss, James Ross, and Larry Tabb

NIC STUCHFIELD: Market quality is not an easy concept to define. As I was searching for a definition, I came across an interesting paper published by one of our keynote speakers Ian Domowitz, and Benn Steil in 1999, from which I quote:

> "In the absence of a precise definition of market equality," Ian wrote back in 1998, "we focus on liquidity, information efficiency and volatility. Liquidity is a multi-dimensional factor, which we address through consideration of the science of the bid-ask spread and measures of market depth. We would concede that all aspects of what we call market quality could ultimately be characterized by the term cost, which is borne by some party in the trading process. This is clear in the case of bid-ask spreads."[1]

With that, I will start by asking Jim a question. In light of developments with dark pools and other changes in market structure on both sides of the Atlantic, please give us your best definition of market quality today.

JAMES ANGEL: The problem with a precise definition is that market quality means different things to different people. Sometimes we look at cost. Sometimes we look at liquidity. For most, market quality is kind of like the distinction between art and pornography: we know the difference when we see it. A cost to one party is revenue to another. The optimal cost is not necessarily zero to the extent that the other party is providing some services for that revenue.

Of course, as a participant on a particular trade, I would like to pay zero commission and have zero market impact. But I would like the market mechanism to provide the service quickly. I would also like the market infrastructure to provide the market information I need. For a trader, cost is one thing. But retail investors generally have different needs. They have different preferences from institutional investors. As a retail investor, I care a lot about the retail bid-ask spread for a hundred shares. An institution cares more about the liquidity for a hundred thousand shares. From the issuer's perspective, it is not necessarily a matter of cost; it is a matter of raising capital. Is the trading system providing enough of a secondary market so that I can

N. Stuchfield (✉)
MTS S.p.A., Rome, Italy

[1]Ian Domowitz and Benn Steil, "Automation, Trading Costs, and the Structure of the Securities Trading Industry", *Brookings-Wharton Papers on Financial Services, 1999.*

R.A. Schwartz et al. (eds.), *Technology and Regulation: How Are They Driving Our Markets?*, Zicklin School of Business Financial Markets Series,
DOI 10.1007/978-1-4419-0480-5_6, © Springer Science+Business Media, LLC 2009

raise capital in the primary market? Can my investors cash out properly in the secondary market? Is the market adequately promoting my securities? That is a very important part of the equity market.

How does a firm get its shares to stand out of the mass of 30,000 publicly-traded companies worldwide, with over 10,000 public companies in the US alone? The issuers face a big challenge of how best to market their securities. There is no single definition of market quality, but we all have a pretty strong sense that markets have improved a lot in the last few years.

STUCHFIELD: Who else on the panel has thoughts about market quality in these very fragmented markets?

LARRY TABB: There is a shift in market structure. Look at London or at Europe, which tend to be very centrally organized, and then look at the US markets, which had become centralized but now in reality are very fragmented. Today, there are six or seven regionals and 35–40 dark pools in the US. Is a central market, where all orders compete together, more efficient than a fragmented market, where competition is essentially between the market centers? There are proponents on both sides of this debate. I believe that a central market is, perhaps, an antiquated idea. In today's market with technology and connectivity, you have orders and competition, as well as market center competition. The market centers are competing on speed, on time, on price and on other issues.

STUCHFIELD: What you are getting at, Larry, is the proliferation of liquidity pools in the US. It is less apparent in Europe, which I would argue, is not as centralized as it appears. Is the proliferation of liquidity pools in the US good for market quality? Bill?

WILLIAM HARTS: As for Europe, once MiFID[2] is fully implemented, you will have scenarios similar to what we have in the US. There will be more competition among marketplaces in electronic and traditional venues. But, as Larry alluded to, electronic trading – algorithmic trading, really – has saved us, in a sense, by bringing liquidity together from many different places. Consequently, having one central marketplace is not nearly as important as it was a few years ago. We need to focus more on transparency among all of the marketplaces. With enough connections and algorithms, having a lot of markets is not necessarily a bad thing any more.

STUCHFIELD: Jim?

JAMES ANGEL: You mean transparency, or connectivity? For dark pools, transparency and connectivity are very different.

HARTS: Yes, of course. When you are talking about market quality, in general, people believe that more transparency means better market quality. That goes back to

---

[2] The markets in Financial Instruments Directive (MiFID), enacted on November 1, 2007, seeks to integrate the European Union's financial markets and, therefore, to promote more cross-border trade executions by ensuring that investors can execute orders with counterparties in other E.U. countries on the same terms as their domestic markets. MiFID includes mandatory pre- and post-trade transparency and capital requirements for financial service firms.

Jim's original definition: traders want to buy at the lowest price, and sell at the highest price, and it will be easier to do that the more prices, in general, that can be seen.

JAMES ROSS: People are talking a lot today about the importance of price discovery. When we talk about market quality, as Jim said earlier, it means different things to different people. My background is in the dark pools and the crossing networks environment. I have not heard much from the panels today about quantity discovery. This is clearly a major component of what is driving ways to bring out the supposed order flow in these hidden pools. As Paul Davis pointed out, these dark pools have actually been around for years. They include Instinet, ITG, and the electronic AZX, or Arizona Stock Exchange, which closed in 2001. In other words, it is not as if we have revolutionized our order-driven markets by suddenly adding hidden or reserve orders. Yet we still do not have a solution, other than what the ATS environment has provided today – a block trading capability from the likes of Liquidnet and Pipeline. But there are no exchange facilities offering a similar trading capability.

In my world of point in time matching and opaque environments, I think about the importance of transparency – and not just anonymity – including the importance of order information. On the dynamics of market quality, I see a tendency to focus on transparent, continuous auction environments, as opposed to other environments that might be more suitable, including a call auction environment. I do not think the exchange model approach is completed. One simple electronic continuous environment is not necessarily the panacea for all the needs of the market participants.

STUCHFIELD: David, can you talk about the derivatives market?

DAVID KRELL: Every market looks at the most efficient way to promote price discovery. The debate in this context is whether the centralized marketplace, where an order is routed to one exchange for execution, is more or less efficient than a decentralized marketplace, such as the foreign exchange market in currencies. Some people would argue that because you can reach many different destinations very quickly with technology, you no longer need physical proximity. In the past, traders had to look at each other every moment on floor-based markets. To some extent we have evolved from that, beginning with ECNs in the mid-1990s. We are now starting to see that in the derivatives market. The fundamental issue on the table today is, what is the ideal market structure to affect price discovery? We want to reach the largest available market with the least disruption. Cost means many things, including the reliability of a system. For example, when volatility increases we see more and more activity because of the reliability of our system.

STUCHFIELD: Are specialists – the liquidity providers – an important component of market quality?

KRELL: On a blank piece of paper in 2000, we started to sketch the ideal market structure for options trading. We felt that having dealers at all times providing their quotes and many different option series was important. We trade options and about 1,500 stock and ETF indexes. This adds up to over 150,000 different issues.[3]

---

[3] As of August 2008, the number of securities had expanded at the ISE to 190,000 along with 200,000 different series of options.

It translates into an awful lot of quotes and quote changes on the ISE as the underlying securities change. It is different on the equities market front where we have, for example, one quote for Google. But we have 460 different series for Google options alone. It is a real challenge to support that. On stock exchanges, speed is one of the most important factors. In the options market, however, it is the ability to simultaneously quote in a group of options; for example, Microsoft options. When the stock changes price, say the price goes up 3 cents, for example, we have to update about 120 different derivatives of that one underlying stock. How do you update all those quotes simultaneously as the stock goes up and down? The challenge in the equity markets is not the same.

HARTS: Why do some market participants feel it is important to have specialists providing some form of continuous liquidity in the options market, but in the cash equities market maybe it is not as important?

TABB: There must be some sort of liquidity provider in the market for options. I do not want to step on any toes in the cash equities markets, but I probably will. We have seen a lot of investment in the US regional exchanges. When they were initially capitalized, it was thought that each would be equal and have similar amounts of market share. But that did not happen. If the regionals combined garnered 6% of overall equity trading it would be surprising, because they have certainly not captured 10–15% of the market. The question then becomes, why did BATS[4] grow and become the biggest, new exchange, even though it is not technically an exchange? For that matter, what attracts market and limit orders to an exchange? If nobody is putting limit orders into an exchange, it is hard to match orders. Limit orders on the book are critical in terms of becoming a successful exchange. That is typically the job of a market maker, a specialist or someone similar.

STUCHFIELD: Bill asked why people talk about the specialists' important role on the options markets compared with the cash equities markets, where they are viewed in a different light. Liquidity provision in any market is important. In London we have worked very hard to encourage liquidity providers to fill the gap that was created by the disappearance of four market makers in 1997. That is when this market making system was converted into the SETS system.[5] It is interesting to watch a lot of non-traditional players, participants like Citadel Investment Group, the hedge fund management firm in Chicago, or quasi-hedge funds, that organized member firms, to informally provide market liquidity in their daily trading activities on exchanges and other venues. It is quite a market-making role. The effect of this is a narrowing

---

[4]BATS Trading, an ECN based in Kansas City, was approved as a registered national securities exchange by the Securities and Exchange Commission in August 2008 when its market share in US stock trading was hovering around 10%.

[5]SETS, or Stock Exchange Electronic Trading System, is an electronic order-driven market combined with market maker liquidity for trading in the FTSE All Share Index, Exchange Traded Funds, Exchange Traded Commodities, as well as more than 180 of the most traded AIM and Irish securities.

over the past 10 years of bid-ask spreads in London. But there is a distinction between the cash equities and the options markets.

KRELL: People often ask me if we have any algorithmic traders in options. All of our primary market makers, and every one of our competitive market makers, has been an algorithmic trader, by definition, because they use computers to generate their quotes. And you cannot update so many options series that rapidly without algorithms. It is impossible.

ROSS: I cut my teeth on the electronic cross network venue,[6] but now being a part myself of the New York Stock Exchange, one thing is clear to me. The New York is definitely aware of the many needs of the market and, therefore, is providing different types of services to satisfy them. How will the specialists perform in this new electronic environment? It is important to have the market maker providing a fair and orderly market in both volatile and non-volatile times. When the business proposition may not be there for the Citadels and the others to provide liquidity, who will replace them? One of the values of a specialist is being willing and available to provide liquidity. Of course, this is in a rapidly evolving world of algorithms and different capabilities. But the NYSE is committed to making sure that someone will be participating in that market, whether or not there is volatility.

STUCHFIELD: Our experience is that in the liquid stocks that is not necessary at all. Speaking as a former market maker myself, I can say that the market makers once acted as a bulwark against the volatility in the market. But what we now have is a much more natural price setting process in which all market participants – including non-members through Direct Market Access, or DMA – can place orders more directly. There is always the price at which a trader or somebody is prepared to enter the market. The market does not get "gappy" in the way that you would expect without the sort of liquidity support that you are talking about. The UK market, like the US, has exhibited much lower levels of volatility over the last 3–5 years than it has in any prior period. So I am not sure that you need formal liquidity structures in liquid stocks like we have had in the specialist system. It is a different ballgame in less liquid stocks.

ANGEL: It depends on the type of instrument. Some stocks are liquid on some days but not on other days. The natural liquidity provision from natural limit order traders, or the fair weather traders, is great when stocks are liquid. But if you want a liquidity provider at other times, there has to be an economic incentive for people to step up to the plate and provide liquidity when it is not economically attractive. If you want to have adequate liquidity for less liquid stocks, or in the less liquid times, provisions must be made in the market mechanism to compensate those liquidity providers.

ROSS: As David Krell said earlier, when they started the ISE, they sat down with a blank sheet of paper and wondered about how to incent people to provide liquidity.

---

[6]From 1989 to 2003, Ross was responsible for the crossing business at Instinet, where he worked for Global Instinet Crossing and managed its domestic and international sales and development.

The ISE obviously did a very good job because it has been tremendously successful. But the New York Stock Exchange specialists are sort of operating at a disadvantage right now. The rules that specialists must follow to participate were written in a different time and place, long before the hybrid market. For all I know, they were written before the advent of electricity (laughter). The New York will have to modify the parameters somewhat so that specialists can operate successfully in the current environment. The current management of the exchange recognizes that and they are making steady progress.

STUCHFIELD: In an extreme sort of sense, if all liquidity existed in dark pools there would surely be a major problem with the price discovery process. At what level of darkness, in terms of market share, do you begin to become uncertain about the price discovery process? Jim?

ANGEL: Price formation could be thought of as a statistical sampling process. A lot depends on the liquidity of the underlying instrument. Almost all of the trading in a very liquid instrument could be done in a dark pool. Once you have a statistically significant sample that everybody can see, you have good price formation. On the other hand, you would still have problems with price formation with a very illiquid instrument even without dark pools.

STUCHFIELD: Any other views on that?

HARTS: Well, whose responsibility is it? Traders are keeping their orders hidden because they think it is in their economic self-interest. I scratch my head and say, "Well, people are complaining about the hidden orders, and about not being able to see what is happening in the market." But those are the same people who want everybody else to display their orders so that they can have an economic advantage. I am not sure that there is a good solution to what you are talking about. As it was noted, dark pools have existed for many years, going back to what we called upstairs trading. In those days you had to pick up a phone and call somebody to find out what their price was in their dark pool. Today, you just ping them with your algorithm.

TABB: Are we getting to a point where displaying liquidity is immaterial? There are reserve orders; there are hidden orders; there are dark pools. There are algorithms that enable a trader to execute 100,000 shares, but I only want to show 500 shares or 200 shares.

STUCHFIELD: That was my point. If there is so much hidden liquidity, in dark pools or in so-called iceberg orders in public exchanges – that is, orders entered into public markets in which the displayed sizes are less than the total order sizes – then the price formation process may be in danger.

TABB: Maybe we need a new market structure where we only show quotes and do not display depth. For example, I want to buy at 02 or 03. How much is there? Who knows? I don't care about depth in this kind of market structure. More than likely the other side of my trade is less than 300 shares and was generated by an algorithm anyway. Nobody wants to display liquidity, or depth today.

ANGEL: Do not forget, we also have post-trade transparency. Within 90 s of seeing a trade, no matter how dark the pool, the rest of the world knows the price at which people are trading. Post-trade transparency has an enormous part to play in the price discovery process.

ROSS: The sky is not falling here. If the liquidity that flows in the dark pools is seen as detrimental to the price formation process, that is more conjecture than reality. You can say it is the tail wagging the dog. For many years, we have been trying to fit quantity sensitive liquidity into a transparent environment. Technology, and regulation to a degree, has come along to give us new options and new opportunities – and now suddenly 40 of these dark pools. But dark pools have indeed been around forever, and they are not going away.

What this signifies is a need to acknowledge the importance of quantity discovery. This does not mean that quantity sits in one pool, and that price discovery sits in another. I am not saying that they necessarily have to exist independently. They certainly may even circle one another. But if you tackle the issue of quantity discovery, you can then find a way to potentially link quantity and price discovery.

We can all say, "May Day and all hell is going to break loose." I do not think that. I believe that the anonymous opaque environment is not the big, bugaboo that we are all making it out to be. This is a great opportunity for us to perform in the marketplace to address an obvious need. In this marketplace we still do not do blocks. Liquidnet and Pipeline do. Let us figure out how we can adapt and evolve this marketplace to embrace that.

STUCHFIELD: The advances that we have made in reduced market impact, and increased liquidity in the markets over the past decade, are both very real. This could not have happened without dicing and slicing processes and complete transparency of pre-trade order desires. Bill talked about MiFID's role in changing the markets in Europe. Some say that MiFID and Reg NMS – as you know, this US regulation seeks to protect orders and overhaul trading here – are in some sense twin sisters. Andreas, what is your perspective on MiFID in Europe, and Reg NMS in the US?

ANDREAS PREUSS: MiFID will affect the European trading markets in much the same way as Reg NMS in the US. The effects in Europe will vary by country. The impact on the German marketplace is likely to be much smaller than the impact on, for example, the French marketplace.

I would like to comment here on dark pools. I agree that they are not a recent development. But technology allows us increasingly to link dark pools at the leisure of the user. A friendly and productive co-existence of the classic exchange markets with very transparent liquidity, and the so-called dark pools, will clearly emerge. Electronic developments have improved the efficiency of markets. I believe that the dark pools will most likely continue to proliferate.

STUCHFIELD: As a fellow European, it would be unreasonable to put you on the spot without being prepared to answer it myself! I very much agree with what you said. The impact of MiFID will be very different in each country. From my perspective, competition is nothing new to the London Stock Exchange. The Financial Services

Authority in the UK has always encouraged competition. Upstairs trading in London is as well developed as it is here in the United States. There has never been a concentration rule in the UK unlike in a number of other European countries. This rule is a national law, or regulation, mandating that orders are routed and executed in a monopolistic public limit order book at an exchange. Consequently, the abolition of those concentration rules, as a result of MiFID, will have a major impact on other European countries, but will not make a difference in the UK.[7]

Ian said earlier that he thought that Reg NMS was a non-event. MiFID, however, will obviously be a catalyst for competition in Europe. London, however, will be, relatively speaking, unaffected for a number of reasons. These include the fact that there is no concentration rule, which means any business can be transacted upstairs, or "off-book," as well as the fact that the regulatory environment in the UK has, for over a decade, positively encouraged competition in the LSE. MiFID will more likely affect the degree of competition rather than the nature of competition. Calvin?

DONALD CALVIN (National Stock Exchange) [From the Floor]: Based on your experience in London, what are your views on Turquoise?[8]

STUCHFIELD: There has been lots of investment bank sponsored competition. You have seen it with the regional exchanges here, in Boston, for example. There have been many instances of investment bank led competition in London as well. For instance TradePoint, before that business was sold to the Swiss to form Virt-x.[9] This is a powerful group of investment banks. They seem to be making a reasonable effort to organize Turquoise so that it will be a reality rather than just a piece of public relations. It needs to be taken seriously. Competition in London is not new; we welcome it. It has always made us leaner and fitter. The London Stock Exchange would never have introduced SETS had it not been for the competition from TradePoint when it was originally set up in the mid-1990s. The market in London today is a lot better because of that competition.

PREUSS: We are also wholehearted believers in competition. We totally welcome the Turquoise initiative and any other similar initiatives. Turquoise and other projects force institutions, and those who organize markets, to think and act competitively throughout their entire process chain. There is one aspect that I remain skeptical of

---

[7]Prior to the implementation of MiFID, France was alone among the three largest E.U. member states which had a "concentration rule" requiring orders to be routed to a national exchange. The other two, the U.K and Germany, had no concentration rule, which helps explain Stuchfield's comment about the impact of MiFID in the UK. Similarly, Preuss, speaking before him, said MiFID's impact on Germany would be less pronounced compared to France. Under MiFID, concentration rules would be swept aside in the E.U. There are no concentration rules in the US.

[8]Turquoise was launched in August 2008, out of London, as an electronic cash equity trading platform, which aimed to undercut existing exchanges with a Multilateral Trading Facility across Europe in hundreds of stocks.

[9]London-based Virt-x, launched in September 2005 as an integrated trading, clearing and settlement system for pan-European stocks, was developed from a platform built by Tradepoint. Virt-x, owned by Switzerland's SWX Swiss Exchange operator, had a 2% market share of trading in European blue chips and a 14% market share when Swiss equities are included, as of December 2007.

(though I might be proven wrong): whenever somebody volunteers to organize a market, and at the same time is an integral part of that market with indisputable vested interests in that market, will it work? Can those who are not part of the consortium be successfully convinced that they can entrust their business to those who are handling it, without those who are handling it ever being able to 100% demonstrate their independence?

Ten years ago, there were several attempts to get BrokerTec,[10] in its original concept, off the ground. One of the fundamental stumbling blocks at the time for BrokerTec, was not so much the idea behind its market model. It was that those who wanted to organize the system wanted to act on both sides of the fence.

STUCHFIELD: As a publicly-owned exchange, we have an absolutely unquestionable mandate to increase the quality of our market. Every time we have increased the quality of our market, such as by improving the fee structure, the market as a whole has benefited. And we ourselves have also gained from the extra volume. I am not saying that this same logic will not apply to Turquoise. But I agree with you, the ownership structure of Turquoise calls into question whether all the members of the Turquoise consortium will always have market quality as their number one objective.

TABB: In the US, the regional exchanges had some challenges in getting their owners to provide liquidity. That is going to be a similar issue in Europe. A lot of orders that come into the exchange from the brokers are market orders. You need somebody who will actually quote. You need a liquidity provider to draw people into the market. Aside from Reg NMS; brokers order routing arrangements; or best execution obligations, brokers are not saying, "We will put all of our orders in Boston, Cincinnati, Chicago, Philly or whatever else." That will be a similar challenge for Turquoise, unless it can find electronic liquidity providers like Lime, GETCO, or Tradebot in the US to quote really tight markets in the UK. It will be hard for new markets to become successful. Some market participants like these electronic brokerages need to populate the order book to attract the majority of the order flow. If there are no participants to populate the book, they will not achieve the critical mass to go head to head with the traditional exchanges.

HARTS: Larry, we have seen instances of that happening, where dealers, or the participants who founded an exchange or an ECN, place their own liquidity in them. Clearly, the original founders of BATS put a lot of their own order flow into BATS. They can do this because they are trading, for the most part, proprietarily. They are not as concerned about how to handle customer order flow, for instance. Once you start worrying about handling customer order flow, it is much harder to say, "I will direct all of my customer orders to venue X because I have an investment in it." That would obviously not be in the best interest of your client. But in terms of your own proprietary, or principal order flow, you can make the choice.

---

[10] BrokerTec, then owned by 14 of Wall Street's bond trading houses, was launched on June 2000 trading cash fixed income products. In August 2002, London-based ICAP purchased Brokertec's Global bond business, which gave ICAP a combination of voice and electronic trading.

HAROLD BRADLEY (Ewing Marion Kauffman Foundation) [From the Floor]: I have heard all day long that brokers are competing with exchanges. I have heard all day long that technology has been the major driver. In every other industry, the emergence of technology has created efficiency, lower profit margins or economic rents, and made it much harder to compete. How many exchanges do we need with the technology eliminating inefficiencies in the market? How do they survive and build a franchise? And, finally, what is in it for the issuer?

ANGEL: The question, "How many exchanges do we need?" is a good one. It is the same question as "How many gas stations do we need" or, "How many supermarkets do we need," to adequately serve customers and provide the benefits of a competitive marketplace. We often forget that the marketplace is not a single institution or trading platform, even though we are focused on the institutions. The market is really the network of all the buyers and sellers who may be interested in trading a particular instrument. The network is the market. Within that network, we have competing exchanges, competing trading platforms, and various intermediaries who link the buyers and sellers together. I would argue that today's market is far less fragmented than it has ever been in history. That is because we have excellent transparency and fast communication, and because the costs to the vendor and to the consumer have fallen dramatically.

BRADLEY: I totally agree, but who is going to make money off of that?

ANGEL: Aren't we all (laughter)?

ROSS: The new dynamic and paradigm here is that exchanges have to really compete. Down through the years, the likes of ITG and other broker-dealers were developing innovative ideas for faster executions and other services in electronic environments. Now with regulatory and technological advances, the exchanges are taking into account a lot more of the capabilities that were available at these brokerages. I come from an incent background where I never got directed order flow. We did not provide capital; we did not offer research. We were an execution-only shop. We had to add value to the execution process. That is what we sold, promoting best execution practices. So we grew our business on functionality and value. Every day I had to offer value. If I did not offer value, I would not run it on the cross. In fact, no one would give me the order. This same mindset has now crossed over to the exchange environment. That will be a very powerful motivator for the exchanges.

STUCHFIELD: Unfortunately, our time is up. I would like you to thank the panel for a very lively discussion.

Chapter 7
Dialog with John Thain

John Thain and Robert Schwartz

ROBERT SCHWARTZ: I am pleased to introduce John Thain. John, I am so glad that you could not attend the conference last year (laughter)! At the time I just saw it as an unintended consequence of your blackout period. But because of that you are here with us today and I am delighted

JOHN THAIN: Yes, and it is my pleasure.

SCHWARTZ: I would like to begin with a comment on some major developments at the New York Stock Exchange. Under your leadership a tremendous amount of change has been happening as the NYSE reengineers itself. You are spearheading these changes in any number of ways. Here are three examples: The introduction of an electronic, order-driven trading system in the NYSE hybrid market; your product line; and the globalization of the exchange. This past year alone your global reach has been extended in several directions. To India where the NYSE Group took a 5% stake in the National Stock Exchange, India's largest exchange. To Japan, where you signed a strategic alliance with the Tokyo Stock Exchange. And, of course, to Europe and the NYSE's merger with Euronext with international headquarters in Amsterdam and Paris. *Voila!*

THAIN: *Bonjour!*

SCHWARTZ: *Comment allez-vous?* How do you do it all? These are massive undertakings. Did you start with a grand vision, or did this sort of evolve?

THAIN: First, I am sorry that I could not be here last year. I am anxiously waiting to see what other consolidations happen in the coming year! So, if you decide to have more than one conference a year these other consolidations could make for interesting topics.

SCHWARTZ: I will let you know!

THAIN: Several factors have led us to make some changes. To begin, look at the markets. They already are global in nature. The market participants, including financial institutions, investment banks, and commercial banks, had already

J. Thain (✉)

R.A. Schwartz et al. (eds.), *Technology and Regulation: How Are They Driving Our Markets?*, Zicklin School of Business Financial Markets Series,
DOI 10.1007/978-1-4419-0480-5_7, © Springer Science+Business Media, LLC 2009

become global. The exchanges were lagging behind in that globalization process for a number of reasons. Exchanges in many parts of the world are still viewed as national assets. They were slow in demutualizing and becoming public, for-profit companies. But as that eventually occurred, it was natural to see them globalize, much like the other markets and financial players had already done.

We are still at the start of this consolidation process. You can expect more conferences like this one. We will see the development of a relatively small number of large, multi-product global exchanges of which we will be one, or will be the leading one. But we will not be the only one. There will also be lots of smaller exchanges. As you know, almost every country in the world has an airline, a flag, and an exchange. It is not hard to create new exchanges. There are new ones being created all the time. We will certainly push for that in Europe. The big picture is that there will be a small number of large, multi-product global exchanges, and lots of little ones, either serving regional or localized markets or starting up.

We have taken the largest market in the US, the New York Stock Exchange, and combined it with the largest cash market in Europe – Euronext. We trade in two of the three main currencies in the world, dollars and Euros. We picked up Liffe,[1] which operates in London. And, as you mentioned Bob, we are moving into Asia, buying 5% of the National Stock Exchange in India, and forming our strategic arrangement with Tokyo. I do not know if this will all occur by your next conference, but we will also position ourselves in China. That will really map out our global marketplace.

The other phenomena driving the world of exchanges is the customer base that increasingly wants to trade instantaneously and electronically and, to some extent, anonymously. That also is driving the push for more electronic trading. The NYSE was slow in allowing more electronic trading to occur at the exchange, despite its growth elsewhere. We have lost market share because electronic players are a large and growing percentage of the market. If we want to maintain our position in that marketplace we must move in this direction.

SCHWARTZ: One of our pet peeves comes from last year's conference. Catherine Kinney[2] said she believed in a centralized model. I too have believed in this for years. Yet, the industry is moving away from a centralized model. We talked today about the dual themes of fragmentation and consolidation. I heard your comments on consolidation. Consolidation has two dimensions. One is spatial, which I have strongly supported. There is also temporal consolidation. As you know, trading in blocks of stock has been replaced with the slicing and dicing of the big orders. Kathy used a colorful phrase here, she called it "slicing and dicing, death by a thousand cuts." My question is, will a centralized market come back? Will the blocks come back?

---

[1] Liffe, the derivatives market based in London, was acquired in January 2002 by Euronext, which subsequently merged with NYSE Group to become NYSE Euronext.

[2] Ms. Kinney, Group Executive Vice President, Head of Global Listings, NYSE Euronext and based in Paris at the time of writing, was previously President and Co-Chief Operating Officer of NYSE Group. (NYSE Group and Euronext were subsequently combined under holding company NYSE Euronext, which was launched on April 4, 2007.)

Also, in the context of your new market structure, would you say a couple of words about MatchPoint?[3] MatchPoint is interesting from the perspective of consolidation in three ways. One, it is pulling together larger size orders. Secondly, it is pulling them together at more specific points in time (that is known as temporal consolidation). Finally, MatchPoint enables portfolio trading. All of those are dimensions within which a market can consolidate or fragment.

THAIN: Your questions raise a lot of important issues. We have seen average trade size continue to decline[4] as slicing and dicing have continued to grow. This is a function of a greater amount of algorithmically-driven trading. We have to respond by offering more and faster electronic access to that centralized marketplace. We have to keep the sliced and diced tranches coming to the NYSE so that we can provide sharper price discovery to the marketplace.

Algorithmic trading will continue to drive much of the overall trading. That trend will not stop. Our goal is to permit more electronic trading, both on the New York Stock Exchange and, of course, through the all-electronic Archipelago (which is very, very fast).

Fragmentation is a concern because most of the dark pools (including crossing networks) still need a centralized marketplace like the New York Stock Exchange to determine what price to cross their trades at. If you move order flow into those crossing networks or darks pools, as the markets fragments, you start to undermine the centralized pricing structure that is needed to support them. So, there is a balance that we must strike between the dark pools and the centralized pricing structure. However, I do not believe that we will eliminate the dark pools. They are a fact of life. But, at the same time, we must make sure that they do not undermine the fundamental price discovery process of a centralized market.

MatchPoint is an attempt to recapture some of those larger blocks that are being crossed off the exchanges. And it will offer a portfolio capability that does not exist anywhere else. The NYSE wants to support our customers. For example, if customers want to discover size, or to trade big blocks in a dark pool, we want to respond to that need. We would much rather have them trade those blocks on an NYSE exchange-driven crossing network than somewhere else.

SCHWARTZ: About 35 years ago, I was at a meeting with William (Mel) Batten[5] when he was Chairman of the NYSE. There was a fascinating discussion about the role of an exchange and what an exchange does. Back then, I was already interested

---

[3] NYSE MatchPoint, the electronic matching facility of NYSE Euronext for aggregated orders at a pre-set time, received regulatory approval from the Securities and Exchange Commission on Jan. 7, 2008. It went live on Jan 22, initially for intraday and after-hour crosses.

[4] The average trade size on the NYSE has continued to decline: to 297 shares by July 2007 and to 225 shares in July 2008, compared with 2,303 shares some two decades earlier. The July 2008 average trade size is calculated from volume at the NYSE, NYSE Crossing Sessions, NYSE TRF and NYSE ARCA, in all stocks traded by the NYSE. Overall, the average US equity trade size in July 2008, including NASDAQ stocks traded outside NYSE Group, was 252 shares, on volume of 211.9 billion shares and 841.8 million trades, according to NASDAQ research.

[5] William Batten was chairman of the New York Stock Exchange from May 1976 until May 1984.

in price discovery. However, I did not speak out at this meeting because I was wondering what others would say. Mel was a good listener. He did not talk much at this meeting, which was organized by the exchange's then chief economist, Bill Freund (who was also present at the meeting and is also with us here today). After a brief pause, Mel quietly said that the NYSE produces "the price." That is, it produces the prices of the securities that are traded on the exchange.

I have been thinking about that today as we discussed the blurry distinctions between brokerage and exchanges, dark pools and other systems. It seems to me that the exchange still does something that nobody else in the market will do. John, you guys discover the price.

There is price discovery, and there is also quantity discovery. The latter occurs largely in the dark pools. How could the two be better coupled so as to better complement each other? After all, the same dark pools that are used for quantity discovery also need price discovery.

Will we get into trouble with block trading if those block trades fragment too much? John, do you see price discovery being undermined? I ask this because I worry about it.

THAIN: No, but I absolutely think that is a risk. If you fragment the market too much, you would undermine the price discovery process. I completely agree with you, Bob. One of the things that we provide is price discovery. The dark pools use exchange-delivered price discovery to set their crossing prices.

Price discovery aside, the exchanges, particularly the New York Stock Exchange, offer something else – liquidity. Of course, there are 40 different dark pools and crossing networks and other systems, but not much stock actually trades in those networks. Consequently, the vast majority of the real liquidity in the market still resides at the exchange. For example, as we put our new Arca system in place, our fill rates have increased to 80%. Not only do we help with price discovery and set the real prices, we are also the place you come to if you truly are a serious trader.

Trading participants run their orders through all these crossing networks, but in the end the trade typically ends up at the exchange. They ultimately trade with the exchange where the liquidity is. So, in this area, we provide two important services: price discovery and liquidity.

SCHWARTZ: Trading professionals like Doreen Mogovero use a term to describe their job. In institutional trading, the challenge is not just to find liquidity. It is to get trading started. I describe NYSE floor traders in this context as "animators" (a term that was previously used in Paris). Doreen calls them "facilitators." The two terms mean the same thing. It is the animation of trading, getting the process going.

Let's turn to technology. This is an increasingly important element of the process I just outlined. This conference is about technology and regulation, and the interaction between them. Last year, we discussed competition, the third catalyst for market structure development. Are technology and competition enough to foster the growth of the markets? Do we really need regulation to prod competition and the application of new technologies?

THAIN: There is no question that competition is driving the market. In my view, there is also no question that technology is also driving the market. Let me explain. The most number of shares that we ever traded was 3.1 billion shares in 1 day.[6] There is no way that you could trade that many shares without our having had tremendous advances in technology. Think back 20 years at the NYSE. Can you imagine trying to handle 3.1 billion shares in one trading day back then? It would not have been possible. Technology is definitely driving the market.

As I understand it, the key to regulation is balance. We need regulation. We need it to ensure that the markets are fair, transparent, and orderly, and that individual and institutional investors can compete on an equal playing field. Of course, while institutions can better protect themselves in the markets, individual investors must not be overlooked.

I do not think that you can say, "gee, just let the market do whatever it wants." Still, we need to strike the right balance so that regulation does not impede the markets. Regulation that prevents positive change, such as new products and new developments, or that impedes their progress, hurts market development. There are concerns about this in the United States today, in contrast to the UK, for instance, where the Financial Services Authority, the FSA, is a much more efficient regulator. They have protections for investors, but they do not impede the development of the market. Currently in the US, the regulatory structure is actually impeding market structure development.

SCHWARTZ: How about some questions from the audience. Joe?

JOE ROSEN (RKA, Inc.) [From the Floor]: In terms of exchange consolidations around the world, what is the magic number of exchanges that will remain? Some observers believe that there will only be 5–7 exchanges in 4 years, because of the economies of scale and the natural monopolies in these arrangements. What is your opinion about this?

THAIN: If that is how you pose the question, the answer will almost certainly be wrong. There will be many more than 5–7 exchanges. For starters, there are exchanges in every country in the world today. Vietnam, for example, has two exchanges. I do not believe that Vietnam's exchanges will consolidate into one global exchange anytime in the next 3–5 years.

The right answer is that there will be a small number of global exchanges. I would actually say probably less than five big global multi-product players. But, in addition, there will be many smaller exchanges, regional as well as new exchanges. After all, you can build a new exchange very easily. The key to success is attracting liquidity.

SCHWARTZ: If this consolidation continues, I will lose sponsors (laughter)! There are tremendous economies of scale, certainly in terms of technology among

---

[6] That record was later eclipsed by the NYSE and NYSE Arca, which have averaged 3.6 billion shares, year-to-date, March 2008. Indeed, subsequent records include 5.1 billion shares traded during one daily session by NYSE Group in July 2007, a record clearly much higher than 3.1 billion.

exchanges. Markets are networks that exhibit very powerful network externalities. In my research, I tend to focus more on the economies of consolidating the flow because I am a major proponent of price discovery. But I would like to differentiate between consolidating the order flow for an individual stock, and including all stocks in a single exchange. Exchanges compete for listings and do not necessarily list the same stocks.

How important listings will continue to be for electronic trading remains to be seen. In any event, exchanges can compete in various ways (which is what you want if the markets are fragmented) while still consolidating the order flow for individual stocks. We are seeing that more in Europe than here because across the Atlantic each country's stock tends to trade in its home country.

THAIN: From an academic perspective, exchanges are a very good example of a business that has a high operating leverage. By this I mean that they have high fixed costs, which is primarily the technology used to run them. But the cost of an incremental trade is almost zero. So they have huge pressures to consolidate. Consolidated trading (say consolidating two separate pools onto a single technology platform) results in huge synergies and efficiencies. There is a tremendous amount of economic pressure to consolidate exchanges onto a single technology platform.

SCHWARTZ: And, as you consolidate, the costs go down and knowledge of the order flow goes up. Bill?

BILL FREUND (Pace University) [From the Floor]: You stressed, John, the importance of multi-product exchanges. I also remember when William Batten was chairman of the New York Stock Exchange. He said he wanted to understand how the New York Stock Exchange could be a one-product store. What plans do you have to convert this one-product store into a multi-product exchange?

THAIN: There is no question about it – we need to be a multi-product exchange. What have we done to achieve this? As you noted, we used to be a one-product store. But with Archipelago, we now trade over-the-counter stocks. We also trade options, and we have a much bigger footprint in exchange-traded funds. Then, with Euronext, we picked up the trading of European stocks. We also picked up another options business, as well as the futures business through Liffe in London. So we are expanding our products.

Why? The derivative businesses – both futures and options – are growing much faster, and they have better margins than the cash business. As a for-profit company, we want to be in those faster growing, higher margin businesses. There also are synergies between these businesses – the ability to trade across products; to trade both the exchange-traded funds and the underlying securities; and to trade stocks and the options written on them. We are also in the process of offering the ability to trade the bonds as well as the stocks of companies – the entire balance sheet of each company. There are probably as many investors today who want to trade General Motors' bonds as well as their stocks. The products with faster growth and better margins that satisfy a broad range of customer demands are driving this.

SCHWARTZ: I was in Europe some years ago and I asked the question, how long does it take to get a closing call auction approved and introduced in Paris? The answer, as I recall, was "in a matter of months." The Americans in the room just could not believe it. They were falling over in disbelief. Chris?

UNIDENTIFIED SPEAKER [From the Floor]: Last year the NYSE announced that it would begin bond trading for every stock listed on the exchange, and that later it would include every subsidiary of those companies. That would generate trading in maybe 10, 12, or a hundred bonds for each stock. How do you see the technology changes that you are using in the stock trading area fitting with the NYSE's Euronext bond trading platforms?

THAIN: Our goal, using Archipelago's technology, is to provide markets in the bonds of our listed companies. Not all of our 2,700 listed companies have bonds that trade, but we will probably make markets in 5,000 or 6,000 bonds. We will try to make the corporate bond market much more transparent. This will make bid-ask spreads tighter and benefit customers who are trading these bonds.

Euronext's bond system, MTS, is a government bond trading system.[7] The ability to expand into corporate bonds is an opportunity for us in Europe, but it is something that we have not explored very much. Right now we are just in the process of launching the US platform.

PAUL DAVIS (TIAA-CREF) [From the Floor]: You mentioned that you have a level playing field for retail and institutional investors, or at least that is your goal. Could you elaborate? It seems that the needs of institutional investors are so different from retail investors. It seems that each needs a different kind of structure.

THAIN: One of the historical structural elements of the New York Stock Exchange is that we allow individual retail investors the same access to prices that the big institutions have, which is not the case in all markets. Many other markets are bifurcated with separate institutional and retails markets, each with its own set of prices. By contrast, on the NYSE, if a retail customer puts in an order to buy 100 shares of IBM while TIAA-CREF is trying to buy half a million shares of IBM, that retail customer is able to compete on an equal basis with the institutional customer.

Our structure is different from most other markets. For instance, if you want to buy many tubes of toothpaste as a big customer, you usually get a different price – a lower price – than what you would pay for one tube at a retail store. We really try to help retail customers have access to the same prices that institutions can get.

DAVIS [From the Floo]: Do the institutions have the same access to prices that retail customers have?

THAIN: Sure. It is one price.

DAVIS [From the Floor]: But you cannot trade half a million shares at one price.

---

[7]In August 2007, NYSE Euronext said it agreed to sell its stake in MBE Holdings to Borsa Italiana. MBE was the joint venture that controlled the MTS fixed-income networks.

THAIN: Actually in the case of IBM, you probably could trade half a million shares at the same price. But it is true that, at some point, size starts to affect the price that you get. Regardless, access to whatever the liquidity is at that instant in time is the same. If there are 50,000 shares offered at a dime, and a retail customer wants to buy a hundred and you want to simultaneously buy all 50,000 of them, you have equal access to those prices.

HAROLD BRADLEY (Ewing Marion Kaufman Foundation) [From the Floor]: There has been a lot of talk today about dark pools. I was kind of taken aback. What hit me is, economically, if these dark pools are springing up, what is New York doing that is wrong? What does it take, through structural changes, to get that order flow back?

THAIN: What you are really saying is, why are these dark pools being created in the first place? Part of the answer is that the economics of trading stocks and trading cash equities has eroded tremendously in the US. If you look at the commissions, or if you look at the profitability of trading stocks, it has become very, very difficult for anyone to make money trading. Blind pools and internalization are one way to try and eke out whatever the bid-ask spread is. If I can capture the bid-ask spread rather than trade it away on a dime on the exchange, that is one way to get a little bit more profitability out of the trade. That is driving some of it.

So too is the ability to trade anonymously. As mentioned earlier, we need to offer better systems to those institutions that want to discover quantity anonymously. Anonymous quantity discovery that is not available on the floor of the exchange is also driving the dark pools.

UNIDENTIFIED SPEAKER [From the Floor]: How quickly do you think the New York will become fully electronic? Is the specialist model today relevant for something the size of New York?

THAIN: As I said previously, I absolutely believe that the specialist model is relevant. If you look at how small-cap stocks trade on the exchange – remember we have 2,700 companies listed – the vast majority are not that liquid. Most stocks trade much better with a specialist providing liquidity.

Stocks trade in a much less volatile way with a market maker like a specialist. Over the last 3 years, we moved 60 companies from NASDAQ (a purely electronic market) to the New York Stock Exchange (a market maker model). The intra-day volatility in the trading of these stocks declined around 40–50%. That is a big difference, not a little difference. The specialists really do add value. They make stocks trade in a less volatile way.

How soon will the exchange be all-electronic? The exchange is almost all electronic today, but a lot of this electronic trading is being handled by the specialists and the brokers on the floor. The percentage of trades done electronically includes the specialists and the brokers. I believe that they will continue to add value, which means that they will continue to be included.

SCHWARTZ: It is possible, I believe, for a specialist to trade within a fully-electronic environment. Michael?

MICHAEL SCOTTI (Traders Magazine) [From the Floor]: Several months ago I heard that the specialists were interested in providing better markets to the issuers, and that they were having discussions about this. However, they were looking for some type of subsidy from the issuers. I do not know if that conversation ever reached the executives in the New York Stock Exchange. Was any movement underway for some type of subsidy, and what do you think about this? The economics of the business would change if there was a subsidy.

THAIN: No, there are no discussions currently in terms of having the issuers themselves provide any subsidies.

GRANT VINGOE (Arnold Porter LLP) [From the Floor]: You talked about regulation slowing things down. This concern was raised with regard to the merger of the NYSE and Euronext. Also, there was resistance in Europe to the SEC regulating foreign companies listing in the US markets. Do you think that the risks of this regulation are exaggerated? Can the non-US companies rest assured that they will be able to participate fully in the US market? Do you have a position on the proposals to allow foreign stock exchanges to operate in the US?

THAIN: Yes, one of the biggest concerns of the Europeans – both the European regulators and the issuers – was for companies listed on Euronext. They were concerned that our transaction would not permit the exportation of trading in these companies in the US markets because of the imposition of Sarbanes-Oxley, and other US rules and regulations. The truth is that those fears were exaggerated. Sarbanes-Oxley only applies to companies that are listed and registered in the US. But the fear was real. We took great pains to educate the European issuers, as well as regulators, that there would be no regulatory overkill, or regulatory creep, outside the United States into Europe.

As a matter of fact, the European regulators entered into a memorandum of understanding with the SEC, each agreeing that they would respect each other's jurisdictions. That dialogue between the US and European regulators has been productive. I also completely support the listing of non-US companies in US markets under non-US GAAP accounting standards.[8] They should not have to conform to GAAP. That issue also led the SEC to be much more responsive to the concept of mutual recognition of foreign regulators. That same mutual recognition could ultimately lead to the trading of foreign company shares in the US that are not registered with the SEC. That would make the markets both more liquid and more accessible, at a lower cost, to all investors. I am very supportive of the developments that are going on right now.

SCHWARTZ: Thank you ever so much, John, for sharing your very important thoughts with us.

---

[8] Generally Accepted Accounting Principals are used in financial accounting, primarily in the US.

Chapter 8
Divergent Expectations[1,2]

Paul Davis, Michael Pagano, and Robert Schwartz

Introduction

In a piece first published in Latin in 1738, the mathematician and scientist, Daniel Bernoulli wrote, " ...the determination of the value of an item must not be based on its price, but rather on the utility it yields. The price of the item is dependent only on the thing itself and is equal for everyone; the utility, however, is dependent on the particular circumstances of the person making the estimate (1954)." The statement is germane to the topic of this paper if one substitutes "expected return and risk" for "utility," and "information set" for "the particular circumstances." This is because an equity's share price is the same for everyone, but each person forms his or her own expectations about the stock's future expected return and risk based on a common information set that people may all have.

Investors who have the same information and interpret it differently are said to have divergent expectations. Financial economists familiar with security pricing have generally frowned on using this assumption, and have alternatively taken the expectations of similarly informed investors to be homogeneous. As implausible as it may be, it is understandable why the profession has taken homogeneous expectations as a cornerstone assumption for much theoretical and empirical analysis – the simplification greatly facilitates the mathematical modeling of financial problems. Furthermore, some academicians consider homogeneity reasonable. After all, give rational decision makers the same information and they should, the thinking goes, reach identical conclusions.

P. Davis (✉)
TIAA-CREF Investment Management LLC, New York, USA

[1] Parts of this paper draw from some sections of "Markets in Transition: Looking Back and Peering Forward," by the same authors, which is the first chapter of a book titled *Banken, Börsen und Kapitalmärkte* (*Banks, Exchanges, and Capital Markets*), Wolfgang Bessler, editor, 2006. We thank Wolfgang Bessler for his comments on an earlier draft of this paper.

[2] Reprinted with permission, from Davis, P., Pagano, M. and Schwartz, R., "Divergent Expectations," *Journal of Portfolio Management,* Volume 34, Number 1, Fall 2007, pp. 84–95. Reprinted in *Journal of Trading*, Volume 3, Number 1, Winter 2008, pp. 56–66.

The homogeneous expectations assumption may be a reasonable modeling device for applications concerning long run inter-stock pricing relationships such as those provided by the capital asset pricing model and arbitrage pricing theory. But reality does not conform to the homogeneous expectations assumption, and many issues concerning market structure and market structure regulation should be analyzed in a divergent (or heterogeneous) expectations context. Our objective in this paper is to consider what this means and what is involved for market participants.

Three decades ago, Miller (1977) took issue with the homogeneous expectations assumption. He writes, "It is implausible to assume that although the future is very uncertain, and the forecasts are very difficult to make, that somehow everyone makes identical estimates of the return and risk from every security. In practice, the very concept of uncertainty implies that reasonable men may differ in their forecasts." In his analysis of the divergent expectations environment, Miller focuses on longer-run pricing implications. Interestingly, he shows that stocks in the highest risk classes can over time yield very low returns. We focus our attention on shorter-run insights concerning market structure, trading, and price discovery.

Despite having experienced over three decades of major structural change in equity markets around the globe, many questions concerning market structure and market structure regulation remain unanswered. Regulatory policy has paid considerable attention to items such as commission rates, bid-ask spreads, transparency, and tick sizes that are important whatever the expectations environment. But regulators have paid scant attention to the accuracy of price discovery and the completeness of quantity (size) discovery. These two issues are of major importance in a divergent expectations environment but in a homogeneous expectations environment do not have particular prominence.

On the academic front, more attention has recently been given to analyzing a divergent expectations environment.[3] Nevertheless, the assumption that investor expectations are homogeneous continues to underlie much market microstructure research on issues ranging from the components of the bid-ask spread and the information content of price changes to the strategic decisions informed traders make to exploit their edge when they have information that is not available to all.

An important example of the homogeneous expectations model is Milgrom and Stokey's (1982) well-known *no-trade theorem*. They show that, in the absence of liquidity traders, no transaction will ever be made even if some investors have new information that would lead them to want to trade with others who do not have this information.[4]

The intuition behind the Milgrom–Stokey result is that any uninformed participant, upon observing the arrival of someone to buy, knows that, with no liquidity traders

---

[3] A number of papers have established that the heterogeneity of expectations can affect market equilibrium prices. See, for instance, Foucault (1999); Handa, Schwartz, and Tiwari (2003); Paroush, Schwartz, and Wolf (2007); and Scheinkman and Xiong (2003).

[4] Liquidity traders are investors who are buying or selling securities to satisfy idiosyncratic cash flow needs (e.g., investing a bonus in a stock or selling securities to make a down payment on a house).

present, the new arrival must know something that would justify shares being valued at a higher price. Thus, the uninformed seller will not accept any price that the informed trader would be willing to pay.

In a Milgrom–Stokey world, all participants (both informed and uninformed) know what the others are thinking, and everyone knows that everyone else knows what everyone is thinking. Consequently, the uninformed will not trade with the informed, and the market will not be viable.

In this rational expectations setting, Grossman and Stiglitz (1976) have shown that, to be viable, an equity market must comprise three types of participants: information traders, liquidity traders, and noise traders. Black (1986) further examines the importance of noise trading, which he identifies as trading on the basis of short-term random fluctuations, or noise, as if it were meaningful information. Momentum players and other market technicians are good examples of these noise traders.

Implicit in the classical trichotomy of information, liquidity, and noise trading is the assumption that all traders in possession of the same information agree on the import of that information. Thus, the expectations of the informed are homogeneous, they translate information into identical share values, and shares have unique values that are determined by the information.

How well does this structure describe real world equity markets? How valuable is the guidance that it gives to market structure development and to market structure regulation? Equity markets are indeed complex institutions; do we know enough about their operations to be able to design them and to regulate them without running afoul of unintended consequences?

We suggest that reliance on a homogeneous expectations-based approach has led to regulation that is well-suited for retail investors (whose trading is commonly motivated by liquidity needs) but has hindered the ability of information motivated institutional investors to trade in large quantities, thus decreasing the market's overall efficiency. Another relevant question is: How far have we come in recent years? We address these and related questions, starting with a brief look at where we are today.

How Far Have We Come?

Technological change and regulatory initiatives have thoroughly reshaped the equity markets, the organizational structure of exchanges, the competitive environment, and the operations of equity traders. Trading volumes have soared, commissions have shrunk, and, although they are difficult to measure, the implicit costs of trading have been lowered, at least in the opinion of many market professionals.

As the twentieth century turned into the twenty first, a new breed of traders has emerged. The young bucks at the trading desks of today have grown up with computer technology. Unlike their predecessors, they are comfortable with the speed and control that a computer can deliver, and they welcome the electronic technology that today is pervasive on buy-side trading desks, in broker-dealer firms, on exchanges, and throughout the alternative trading systems (ATSs).

Surveying these developments, a student of the market might conclude that great progress has been made. It might appear that we have gone much of the way to the promised land.

Not so fast. Over the past 30 years, many questions have been raised and issues debated, but the debates continue unabated and important questions remain unanswered. It is true that today small orders for large cap blue-chips present no problem; they can be executed with lightning speed at current prices. But big orders for stocks of all market cap sizes and all orders for mid- and small-cap stocks are not easily dealt with.

New block trading facilities like Liquidnet and Pipeline have come into being and are attracting appreciable order flow, but they currently account for only a small fraction of total trading volume. Electronic call auctions are being widely used to open and close markets, but their potential for handling institutional order flow has not been adequately exploited. Regulators on both sides of the Atlantic call for transparency but, while they might require that certain orders be exposed, it ultimately is not possible to legislate transparency. Markets have consolidated on both sides of the Atlantic, a trend that will no doubt continue, but regulatory authorities fear the advent of monopoly power even as new players such as Liquidnet and Pipeline emerge.

There are further issues. Best execution, a regulatory requirement in the United States that was first set forth in the 1975 Securities Acts Amendments, is now slated for the European arena with the coming implementation of the Markets in Financial Instruments Directive (MiFID) – but best execution is virtually impossible to define and very difficult to implement. Soft dollar arrangements remain unsavory in the opinion of many, but a forced unbundling of trading, research, and other soft dollar products can have its own undesirable consequences. With computerized order handling and trade execution, speed is now measured in milliseconds, but trading remains a zero-sum game and it is difficult to understand how traders as a community can benefit from operating in a continuous market environment with subsecond response times. Would we all be better off if everybody used Formula One racing cars for commuting and daily shopping trips?

While markets to some extent may have consolidated in places, they are fracturing temporally as large orders are increasingly being sliced and diced and fed to the markets one small tranche at a time. Average trade size on the New York Stock Exchange in 1988 was 2,303 shares; by June, 2005, average trade size had fallen to 343 shares. NYSE block-trading in 1988 represented 2% of reported volume; by June 2007, block trading had declined to 20%. Trading information in general, and quotes in particular, can change with startling speed as fast computerized markets, which means that traders need to have new tools at their disposal. Accordingly, a great deal of attention has turned to algorithmic trading (or *algos*).

Yet one might question whether the widespread use of algos represents a valuable step forward for traders as a group, or whether it is a symptom of continuing friction, illiquidity, high market impact costs, accentuated intraday volatility, and fuzzy pricing in our markets.

What Motivates Trading?

A critical starting point for thinking about market microstructure is a deceptively simple question: What motivates individuals to trade? How good can our understanding of the markets be if we cannot properly answer this very basic question?[5]

As we have noted, the classical academic answer is that there are three types of traders – information, liquidity, and noise traders – and informed traders have the same (homogeneous) expectations about the returns that a stock will deliver. Four major conclusions follow from the homogeneity assumption:

- Information maps uniquely into security values. To say this another way, securities have intrinsic (i.e., true or fundamental) values that are uniquely linked to the information set.
- Stocks prices that diverge from intrinsic values will be driven back to their fundamentals by arbitrageurs. Arbitrage is a key mechanism in both the capital asset pricing model and arbitrage pricing theory.
- If all participants are "informed" (i.e., know the full information set),and trades are triggered for liquidity reasons only, shares will trade at bid and ask quotes that are appropriate given the intrinsic values, and, aside from the bid-ask bounce, prices will follow random walks with drift.
- Informed participants will never trade with each other because they have the same expectations; consequently, liquidity and noise traders must be present for a market to be viable.

But homogeneity is only an assumption, and the four points fit poorly with reality. Accordingly, academic belief that investor expectations based on a common information set are homogeneous has been tempered of late. It is recognized that some participants have private information (namely that they process information so as to gain insights that are not immediately apparent). One striking illustration was reported in the *Wall Street Journal* on October 6, 2003. As summarized by Schwartz, Francioni, and Weber (2006),

> "The *Journal* reported that between June and August 2003 certain large institutional investors, using two detailed pharmaceutical databases that cost subscribers between $25,000 and $50,000 a year, were able to determine that the drug company Schering–Plough was losing market share for its hepatitis C medicine to a competitor, Roche Holding AG. The investing public got hints of the development in July, but full information was not available until August 22. During this period, Schering's share price peaked at $20.47 on June 18 and then drifted down, dipping below $17 as July turned into August…on August 22, the day when Schering confirmed the declining sales trend for its product, shares opened down $2.18 at $14.30."

Whether participant expectations differ because of the actual "production" of private information as in the Schering–Plough case, or simply because different people interpret information differently, the expectations of a group of investors can

---

[5] For further discussion of the motives for trading, see Sarkar and Schwartz (2007).

be divergent. A spectrum of market realities call attention to the importance of understanding this reality:

- Information sets are vast and enormously complex, and our tools for analyzing them are relatively crude. Consequently, precise assessments and translations into exact share values are not possible. Imprecision on this front leads to disagreements about share value.
- Analysts' recommendations commonly differ.
- Much short selling is no doubt triggered when participants disagree with market assessments of share values.
- Institutional investors commonly execute large trades (100,000 shares or more) in individual stocks with each other. Trading in new automated trading systems such as Liquidnet or Pipeline offers compelling evidence of large institution-to-institution trades. These trades are not likely to be motivated by liquidity needs (lists or basket trades would be used for that). Participants are also unlikely to be noise traders. Thus, they must be information traders who disagree with one another about share value.

With divergent expectations, trades are not made simply because some participants have superior information while others are experiencing idiosyncratic cash flows (the liquidity traders), and yet others believe that they have detected exploitable patterns in the data (the noise traders). Rather, participants may trade with each other simply because they disagree with each other. Such trading may occur as a natural part of the dynamic price discovery that occurs following any news release, and can explain the volume surges that we see then.[6]

If participants are free to disagree with each other, then they are free to change their expectations for their own individual reasons. This reality sheds a different meaning on the term *liquidity trading*, as well as on the divitation between liquidity and information trading.[7] Furthermore, along with being free to change their expectations idiosyncratically, participants may also be influenced by what they observe others are thinking and doing. Paroush, Schwartz, and Wolf (2007) refer to this as adaptive valuation.

From Divergent Expectations to Adaptive Valuations

Once we allow for divergent expectations, a further reality of the marketplace can be recognized: if individuals can form different expectations when faced with common information, then each may be influenced by the decisions of others.

---

[6] For further discussion, see Paroush, Schwartz, and Wolf (2007).

[7] Note that asymmetric information can still be present in a divergent expectations framework. That is, some traders might actually have better information than other traders, and they will be able to trade with less-informed liquidity and noise traders, as well as with each other, if their expectations based on the superior information are different. In this sense, the traditional division of informed, liquidity, and noise traders can be viewed as a special case of the divergent expectations framework.

That is, they may have *adaptive valuations*.[8] Paroush, Schwartz, and Wolf (2007) [PSW] have modeled trading and price discovery in an environment that is characterized by both divergent expectations and adaptive valuations. They assume that any *i*th individual's assessment of share value is a function of two things (1) the publicly available information set and (2) the aggregate assessment of others (which they represent by the proportion of participants who are relatively bullish).

With divergent expectations and adaptive valuations, participants will trade with each other in the absence of information advantages and liquidity considerations. And the very process of trading affects participant assessments and share values. In this environment, as PSW show, shares do not have unique equilibrium values (and they certainly do not have unique intrinsic values). Rather, we are now in a framework where price discovery is a path-dependent process. In such an environment, the behavioral responses of participants acquire importance.

Assume, for example, that 100 participants are each placing a bet on the number of jelly beans in a jar (which holds 2,500 beans). Each participant views the jar individually, and then each steps forward, one at a time in random order, to state a guess that is then revealed to everybody. As the betting proceeds, participants are free to adjust their estimates based upon what they hear the others guessing. Consider the bet that the 31st participant would place when his or her initial guess is 1,800 beans and the average bet of the previous 30 participants is 2,700 beans. We expect that the 31st participant's bet will be a weighted average of 1,800 (her original guess) and 2,700 (the average guess of 30 others).

In this illustration, the large jar of 2,500 jelly beans represents an information set that, because of its size, is difficult for each individual to assess with precision. The bets of the first 30 participants represent price discovery inputs to that point, and the response of the 31st participant to the collective valuations of the first 30 represents adaptive valuations. It can be shown that, as the betting progresses, the collective guess will eventually converge on a value that we might refer to as an equilibrium or consensus value.

Interestingly, if the first participants to arrive happen to place low bets, the equilibrium converged on will be relatively low. Conversely, if they happen to place high bets, the equilibrium converged on will be relatively high. Accordingly, the game is a path-dependent process.

The path-dependent environment differs appreciably from a classical marketplace made up of informed, liquidity, and noise traders, which is characterized by homogeneous expectations among the informed and described as a unique equilibrium process that is not path-dependent. In the divergent expectations, adaptive valuation, environment:

---

[8] The literature on information cascades has also recognized that investors can have adaptive valuations. For example, if several buyers consecutively enter a market and bid up a security's price, then others observing this activity might follow suit and thus form an information cascade (i.e., the trading actions of earlier traders cascade to later traders). This behavior can lead to speculative bubbles and crashes when there are divergent expectations about other traders' valuations. For further details on information cascades, see Anderson and Holt (1996, 1997) and Ball and Holt (1998).

- Information sets do not map into unique security valuations in a deterministic manner that is independent of market processes.
- Price discovery (e.g., finding an equilibrium or consensus value) is a complex and dynamic process; this is not the case in a homogeneous expectations environment where informed participants know true values.
- Elevated short-term (intraday) price volatility can be more richly understood.
- Tools related to technical analysis and algorithmic trading can acquire value.
- Achieving acceptably accurate price discovery becomes an important public policy issue, along with lowering commissions and shrinking the size of bid-ask spreads.
- The clarity of information release has heightened value, along with the speed and fairness of information disclosure.
- The seeds of longer-period bubbles and crashes may be found in the dynamic intraday process of price discovery.
- Price discovery has a psychological or behavioral component (i.e., what signals do participants look at to infer what each other is thinking, and how do they respond to these signals?).
- Noisy price discovery is associated with incomplete quantity discovery (i.e., the difficulty that large trading counterparties have in finding each other and trading the total number of shares that they are looking either to buy or to sell).

Basically, replacing the fundamental simplifying assumption of homogeneous expectations with the more realistic assumption that participant expectations are divergent and adaptive can profoundly impact our thinking about how markets operate. Further investigation of the divergent expectations, adaptive environment should shed useful new light on a spectrum of market structure and public policy issues that continue to remain unresolved.

A Buy-side Perspective on Quantity Discovery

Assets under management run the gamut from a few thousand dollars under the control of one individual to a few million dollars handled by a small fund to many billions of dollars managed by a large institution. As a consequence, and recognizing small retail orders and large orders that are commonly sliced and diced, an equity market network must be flexible enough to accommodate orders ranging from 100 shares to 1 million shares or more.[9]

With 100-share orders, a market maker can set bids and offers, trade across the spread, and make money by capturing the spread, as has been analyzed extensively in the academic literature. A market maker will trade 100 shares all of the time,

---

[9] The full market network is much more than the stock exchange. It includes brokers who have trading desks that compete with stock exchanges. Alternative trading systems are also part of the market network.

1,000 shares most of the time, and 10,000 shares some of the time. We are in a different world when really large orders (100,000 shares and more) are entered in the marketplace.

There are two fundamentally different approaches to trading a large order (like a 1 million-share buy order). First, a trader may slice and dice the order and feed it to the market one small tranche at a time. This approach is motivated by the fundamental design of an order-driven electronic market – a so-called fast mrket. Yet, as we point out in Davis, Pagano, and Schwartz (2006b), when an order is sliced and diced, its complete execution may take quite a while. In other words, while the individual tranches are executed speedily in a fast market, the full order itself is executed slowly.

The second approach is to use the full search capabilities of the market network to find a natural seller to take the other side of the transaction. If participant expectations are divergent, such a search is more likely to be successful. The seller may also be slicing and dicing. Or, the seller may not yet be active in the market, but can be planning to enter soon if conditions are suitable. Knowing that a buyer available can give the seller an incentive to step into the market and trade. Or, perhaps the seller is not in the market because it does not want to sell at the present market price, but would be willing to sell at a premium. The buyer may be willing to pay the premium so as to execute the entire order speedily. A seller might also be found at an ATS like Liquidnet or Pipeline, at a broker's trading desk (using either dealer capital or the broker's knowledge of potential contras), at a crossing network, or at an exchange's call auction. Searching for, and finding, the contra-side of a large order has been called *quantity discovery*.[10]

Ideally, quantity and price discovery should go hand-in-hand, as they do in traditional classroom presentations of demand and supply analysis. The structure of a marketplace is an often overlooked factor with regard to achieving an ideal price and quantity solution. An electronic order-driven market – the central marketplace in most countries – must be augmented by other market mechanisms so as to meet the needs of large buyers and sellers. As additional mechanisms come into play, price discovery and quantity discovery usually become de-coupled. Consequently, price discovery typically occurs at the central marketplace; quantity discovery gravitates to a facility more suitable for institutional trading; and the off-board (or off-book) facility typically free-rides on the prices delivered by the central marketplace.

Implications for Market Structures and Networks

The availability of limit orders and/or market maker bids and offers breaks down for large orders such as a 1,000,000 share buy order. Yet, the full market network is robust enough to accommodate the order.

---

[10] For a further discussion of quantity discovery, see Davis, Pagano, and Schwartz (2006a); Chakraborty, Pagano, and Schwartz (2006); and Sarkar and Schwartz (2007).

What is going on? The divergent expectations hypothesis can shed light on how the big orders are able to get executed. Let's look at an example. Assume a broker works the order as agent, finds the contra side, and brings the natural buyer and the natural seller together. What is motivating the buyer? What is motivating the seller? Most likely, neither the big buyer nor the big seller is a noise trader or a liquidity trader. There is a simpler, more straightforward answer: The buyer has a relatively high valuation, and the seller has a relatively low valuation.

The contra-side traders may find one another in an ATS such as Pipeline or Liquidnet. Large orders traded on these systems are generally not from liquidity traders, and presumably they are never from noise traders. By focusing its system on the needs of buy-side customers, Liquidnet does not include sell-side market makers (who could be seeking to trade to rebalance their inventories in specific stocks). Accordingly, the classic trader division breaks down in this market environment. This leads us to replace the homogeneous expectations assumption with the divergent expectations assumption. That is, we presume that the large trade in a single stock results from a natural buyer with a relatively high valuation meeting a natural seller with a relatively low valuation, and the two of them implicitly agree to disagree.

In keeping with reality, divergent expectations imply a more diverse set of traders than does the classical framework. There are informed buyers and informed sellers, as well as liquidity and noise traders. The informed buyers and informed sellers could be retail-sized investors or institutional-sized investors. Across all of them, expectations can be divergent, and the more diverse reasons for trading most likely lead to better, more robust markets. But order size disparity can have consequences.

Consider a large institutional buy order sliced and diced within a purely electronic order-driven market. A simple adaptive valuations framework counts the number of bulls and bears. What if there is one big bull executing orders hundreds of times? The one big bull often cannot be distinguished from hundreds of little bulls, each buying just once. The sequential trades triggered by the multiple tranches of the big bull's order result in higher prices that can either (1) be justified, (2) lead to a bubble, or (3) be ephemeral and lead to increased volatility. A market network that offers institutions more options than a pure electronic order-driven market to meet counterparties can provide the institutional bull with a benefit by giving less weight to this investor in determining prices.

Off-Book Trading and the No-Trade Theorem Revisited

Price discovery and quantity discovery have traditionally been thought of as occurring within a single trading platform. In fact, they are two distinct functions, and they can become bifurcated. Over 200 years ago, referring to a little assembly line in a tiny pin factory, Adam Smith noted that economic gains can be reaped from a division of labor (i.e., assigning individual workers different specific tasks). An ATS operating side-by-side with a major market center is a classic replication of Adam Smith's pin factory, albeit on a vastly larger scale.

Namely, institutional traders can go to an alternative, less transparent, exchange, meet each other, and trade at lower cost. The alternative site provides quantity discovery, while free-riding on the price discovery services provided by the security exchange's main trading platform.

In the US, quantity discovery is increasingly taking place through ATSs such as Liquidnet (which for the third quarter of 2007 averaged 54.6 million shares a day double-counted, with an average trade size of 52,313 shares) and Pipeline (which for the same period averaged 30.9 million shares a day double-counted, with an average trade size of 37,804 shares). The unbundling, or bifurcation, of price and quantity discovery is occurring in both the US and Europe, but it is difficult to go beyond anecdotal evidence to pin this down, because it is not easy to determine how much trading takes place off-book.

Beyond the US experience, consider Deutsche Börse's main electronic trading platform, Xetra. Currently, there is no trade reporting requirement in Germany, so the actual amount of off-book trading in German stocks is not known. To gain further insight into the matter, we have obtained data from Clearstream's Cascade settlement instructions database for 160 actively traded German equity shares for the month of January 2006 and the period July 2003 through June 2005.[11] (Clearstream is Deutsche Börse's clearing and settlement organization.)

On-book trading is predominantly fast market activity directed to the Xetra electronic trading facility.[12] Off-book trading includes exchange trading that does not go through Xetra or the physical trading floors, as well as upstairs trading in banks, brokerage firms, and ATSs.

We have computed the euro value of trades that do and do not go through the order book for each of the 160 companies that make up the four major German stock indexes: the 30 DAX large-cap stocks, the 50 midcap MDAX stocks, the 50 small-cap SDAX stocks, and the 30 TECDAX technology stocks. For all 160 stocks, the equally weighted percentage amount of on-book trading was 54% for January 2006 and an almost identical 56% for the July 2003 through June 2005 period.

For the July 2003–June 2005 period, the euro trading volume that occurred on-book was relatively small (41%) for the 30 large-cap DAX stocks, roughly half (48%) for the midcap stocks, a clear majority (65%) for the smaller-cap stocks, and yet more substantial for the smaller TECDAX stocks (68%).[13]

These averages indicate that larger-cap stocks trade more heavily off the book, and that small-cap stocks trade more heavily on the book. The finding is intuitively reasonable. Large institutional investors (who are typically more active in the

[11] We are grateful to Robert Urtheil and Miroslav Budimir for making these data available to us. Deutsche Börse has also provided us with guidance on constructing a proxy for off-order book activity. We use this to estimate the relative amount of on-book trading. See Davis, Pagano, and Schwartz (2006a) for more detail on the German data and the adjustment methodology used in the analysis.

[12] Most trading goes through the electronic platform, but the German order book data also include trades executed on Germany's physical trading floors.

[13] Given the small number of observations in our sample, we did not attempt to test the statistical significance of the across sub-sample differences.

larger-cap issues) are less likely to direct their block orders to the book. Additionally, retail orders for these larger-cap stocks are more likely to be netted against each other and internalized by German banks and brokers.

One might expect more free-riding when institutional investors, retail clients, and their brokers have more confidence in the exchange-discovered prices. The greater total order flow for the large-cap stocks translates into more liquid markets and sharper exchange-delivered price discovery. Hence, there may be more free-riding for these stocks. Thus, in the classical tradition of Adam Smith, a "division of labor" appears to be operating in the German market in general, and in the large-cap sector of the market in particular. Price discovery is taking place on-book and, to an appreciable extent, quantity discovery is occurring off-book.

What does this imply about the informed, liquidity, and noise trader trichotomy, and the no trade theorem? The prevalence of off-book trading in a major technologically advanced market conveys an important message to students of the equity markets concerning participants' motives for trading, because participants with different trading motives cluster differently in the standard on-exchange and off-exchange environments.

A more diverse group meets at an exchange: small retail and large institutional customers, liquidity traders, information traders, and momentum players. Participants who trade away from the exchange do so for specific reasons that can make the off-exchange composition of the individual liquidity pools less diverse. Retail orders can be executed upstairs by a bank or brokerage house that nets customer orders; the netting process brings predominantly small liquidity traders together. Large institutional orders are executed upstairs by a block trader or by an ATS speedy execution or to minimize market impact costs.

ATSs such as Pipeline and Liquidnet receive many large single-stock orders, and basket trading is not common on either facility.[14] The sell-side broker-dealer firms are excluded from Liquidnet, and, according to company sources, they direct very little proprietary trading to Pipeline. Thus, for the most part, these two ATSs receive orders that are highly unlikely to be placed by either liquidity or noise traders.[15] Consequently, according to the no-trade theorem, Liquidnet and Pipeline should not be viable – yet they are: average daily trading volumes of 54.6 million shares and 30.9 million shares, and their average trade sizes are 52,313 and 37,804 sahres.

A 52,000-share buy order meeting a 50,000-share sell order for an individual stock at the same moment in time in Liquidnet is very likely the result of two large information-motivated institutional participants coming together to trade with each other. This is particularly strong prima facie evidence that much trading is in fact being driven by divergent expectations.

---

[14] Trade prices are negotiated in Liquidnet, and so a list would have to be negotiated one stock at a time. This is a tedious process and is done only occasionally.

[15] The minimum order size in Pipeline for a large cap stock is 100,000 shares.

Implications for Market Structure Regulation

Market structure regulation has two over-riding objectives. The first is to improve market efficiency, in terms of the containment of trading costs. To this end, major attention has been given to reducing commissions, bid-ask spreads, and market impact costs. Our discussion underscores the importance of including two additional efficiency factors – increasing the accuracy of price discovery and the completeness of quantity discovery.

The second regulatory objective is to ensure fairness across participants by establishing a level playing field. One way in which fairness may be achieved is by regulating information release. For instance, Regulation FD (Fair Disclosure) in the United States, adopted by the Securities and Exchange Commission in 2000, prohibits a company from leaking news to preferred investors.

The fairness concept has also been applied to ensure that one class of investors, small retail customers, is not disadvantaged by a larger, more powerful, and presumably more sophisticated class, institutional customers. It has been pointed out that these two classes are not so distinct in that pension and mutual funds themselves represent large numbers of small investors. More to the point, it is not at all clear that large funds have an information edge over serious retail investors. And, on the contrary, when it comes to total trading costs, it is the retail investor who frequently has an advantage.

A potential buyer of 1 million shares and a potential buyer of 100 shares may have the same high valuation. The buyer of 100 shares can reach out to a national exchange or any other component of the market network to consummate the transaction. The buyer of 1 million shares will have a far more difficult time executing the order. Given the high execution costs incurred by multi-billion dollar pension, mutual and hedge funds, their *raison d'être* for size must lie elsewhere, and it does. A fund's comparative advantage lies in constructing, managing, and monitoring portfolios that meet the fund's objectives and investor desires. The institutions bring disciplined approaches that balance expected return, risk, and liquidity in light of a fund's objectives. Regulators need to be sensitive to these basic institutional functions, the required concomitant trading, and the total cost of trading.

Regulators have also considered fairness in terms of the relative economic strengths of clients represented by investment institutions, and of intermediaries that, in handling orders and providing dealer capital, stand between the ultimate contra sides to a trade. The transfer of wealth between investors and intermediaries is substantial. We should consider this transfer in the context of participant expectations.

The homogeneous expectations hypothesis implies, on average, a triple win–win–win situation for liquidity traders, informed participants, and intermediaries. As trades are made, liquidity needs are met, informed positions with their anticipated future profitability are put into place, and intermediaries are paid for bringing buyers and sellers together. The divergent expectations hypothesis on the other hand suggests that many trades are between informed participants who interpret news differently.

For these trades, the future will reveal which of the contras wins and which loses, while intermediaries, on average, continue to win.[16] This divergent expectations view is far more consistent with observed institutional investment performance: Big funds, on average, do not consistently over time have an informational advantage. What does this imply about regulatory policy?

The past three decades have seen a succession of regulatory initiatives: the Congressional mandate that abolished fixed commissions and called for the development of a National Market System (the 1975 Securities Acts Amendments); the institution of a best execution requirement (the 1975 Amendments); the SEC's Order Handling Rules (introduced in 1997); the removal of the NYSE's off-board trading prohibition, Rule 390 (in December 1999); the change from fractional to decimal pricing which lowered the minimum tick size to one penny (in 2001); and a trade-through prohibition (a principal component of the SEC's Regulation NMS which, went into effect in 2007). Each of these can be viewed as an attempt to lower the explicit costs of trading, principally commissions and effective bid-ask spreads.

The public policy debates concerning these issues and their eventual translation into market structure have not, to our knowledge, been explicitly discussed in terms of the homogeneity, or divergence, of participant expectations, although the homogeneity assumption has been an *eminence grise* behind them. Consequently, not much attention has been given to price and quantity discovery. Why should it be, if shares are thought to have unique fundamental values?

The complexities of price and quantity discovery can be appreciated only when it is recognized that expectations are not homogeneous. Unfortunately, if price and quantity discovery are not adequately taken into account, optimal trading networks will not emerge, and costs will be unduly high, particularly for institutional customers. For example, the current US securities exchanges are well-designed for retail investors but this market structure makes it difficult for institutional investors to place large orders in an efficient manner. Thus, these institutional investors are increasingly choosing to trade on off-exchange systems. This, in turn, exacerbates the bifurcation between price and quantity discovery. Intermediaries too may suffer, although they will continue to find ways to bring buyers and sellers together, even if at higher cost. Consequently, the regulatory debates should take these first principles of market microstructure into account. Only then will we be able to achieve a network that enhances efficiency for the broad market.

---

[16] Moreover, dealers are in one regard "informed" participants with expectations that may differ from those of their customers. Their expectations, however, apply primarily to reading the information in the order flow rather than in the asset's fundamentals. The dealer's risk profile and relationship with a client are further factors that are taken into consideration. The dealer typically does not have a strong opinion about a stock but will still deal. When it sells shares to a 100,000-share bullish buyer, the intermediary is hoping that it will soon be buying 100,000 shares from a bearish seller. Thus, the dealers, as intermediaries, may themselves depend on their own customers having divergent expectations.

There is More Than One Game in Town

Characterizing participant expectations might appear academic and esoteric. Indeed, market structure and public regulatory policy are rarely discussed in terms of the homogeneity or divergence of participant expectations. We suggest that they should be. Unfortunately, academic analysis has, for the most part, assumed that the expectations of the informed are homogeneous and, accordingly, that stocks have unique fundamental values.

The standard asymmetric information dealer models are based on the assumption that some informed traders receive information before others who are uninformed, and that all investors who are identically informed have identical (homogeneous) expectations. Such asymmetry of information can explain dealer bid-ask spreads [see Bagehot (1971) for an early discussion]. Consequently, major attention has been given to items such as bid-ask spreads and tick sizes, while the broader complexities of price discovery and quantity discovery go practically unrecognized. While homogeneous expectations may be a necessary and reasonable assumption for some theoretical modeling purposes, they do not characterize real-world markets. More critically, analyses of real-world markets that are based on the homogeneity assumption can yield misleading answers.

The motive of institutions executing big blocks is almost always information. But a market driven only by trading based on news that everyone assesses identically is not viable, as Milgrom and Stokey (1982) demonstrate. We therefore ask what explains institutions seeking to trade individual securities with each other in large amounts. We suggest the answer is that they do not interpret news identically. Their expectations, in other words, are divergent. While taking market prices into account, some portfolio managers form relatively bullish expectations and wish to buy, while others form relatively bearish expectations and wish to sell.

A buyer can know that a seller is looking to trade because of his or her own valuation, and the seller can know the same about the buyer. Each is willing to trade with the other nevertheless because each has sufficient confidence in his or her own divergent expectation. In effect, the participants are implicitly agreeing to disagree about share value. We suggest that agreeing to disagree in a divergent expectations environment should replace the homogeneous expectations framework used in many microstructure applications.

Comprehending the role played by divergent expectations goes to the heart of two questions – what drives trading, and why does market structure matter? Trading is driven, not by a simple division of informed, liquidity, and noise traders, but also by participants who value shares differently, who are influenced by each other's opinions and actions, and who may revise their individual expectations at any time. Market structure matters because price and quantity discovery are complex processes. They are complex because shares do not have unique fundamental values, and precise fundamental values do not exist because investor expectations are not homogeneous. Rather, because of the vast and enormously complex information sets that asset managers deal with, investor expectations are divergent.

Ultimately, it is the complexity of fundamental information that drives the array of market structure issues that we face today. Consequently, for both market structure design and market structure regulation, we might benefit from paying more attention to how asset managers in the face of imprecise information form different opinions about share values.

References

Anderson, L.R., and C.A. Holt, 'Classroom Games: Information Cascades,' *Journal of Economic Perspectives* 10 (1996), 187–193.

Anderson, L.R., and C.A. Holt, 'Information Cascades in the Laboratory,' *American Economic Review* 87 (1997), 847–862.

Bagehot, W., (pseud), 'The Only Game in Town,' *Financial Analysts Journal* 8 (1971), 31–53.

Ball, S.B., and C.A. Holt, 'Classroom Games: Speculation and Bubbles in an Asset Market,' *Journal of Economic Perspectives* 12 (1998), 207–218.

Bernoulli, D., 'Exposition of a New Theory on the Measurement of Risk,' *Econometrica* 22 (1), 23–36, first published in 1738.

Black, F., 'Noise,' *Journal of Finance* 41 (1986), 529-543.

Chakraborty, A., M.S. Pagano, and R.A. Schwartz, 'Bookbuilding,' *Working Paper*, New York, NY: Baruch College, 2006.

Davis, P., M.S. Pagano, and R.A. Schwartz, 'Markets in Transition: Looking Back and Peering Forward,' in W. Bessler, ed., *Banken, Borsen und Kapitalmarkte (Banks, Exchanges, and Capital Markets)*, Berlin: Duncker & Humblot, 2006a.

Davis, P., M.S. Pagano, and R.A. Schwartz, 'Where are Trades Made in a Fast Market Environment? Life after the Big Board Goes Electronic,' *Financial Analysts Journal* 62 (2006b), 14–20.

Foucault, T., 'Order Flow Composition and Trading Costs in a Dynamic Order Driven Market,' *Journal of Financial Markets*, 2 (1999), 99–134.

Grossman, S., and J. Stiglitz, 'Information and Competitive Systems,' *American Economic Review*, 66 (1976), 246–253.

Handa, P., R.A. Schwartz, and A. Tiwari, 'Quote Setting and Price Formation in an Order Driven Market,' *Journal of Financial Markets*, 6 (2003), 461–489.

Milgrom, P., and N. Stokey, 'Information, Trade, and Common Knowledge,' *Journal of Economic Theory*, 26 (1982), 17–27.

Paroush, J., R.A. Schwartz, and A. Wolf, 'Stock Price Volatility, Price Discovery, and the Endogeneity of Fundamental Values,' *Working Paper*, New York, NY: Baruch College, 2007.

Sarkar, A., and R.A. Schwartz, 'Two-Sided Markets: Insights into Trading Motives,' *Working Paper*, New York, NY: Baruch College, 2007.

Schwartz, R.A., R. Francioni, and B.W. Weber, *The Equity Trader Course*, New York, NY: Wiley, 2006.

Scheinkman, J., and X. Wei, 'Overconfidence and Speculative Bubbles,' *Journal of Political Economy*, 111 (2003), 1183–1219.

Participant Biographies

Leonard Amoruso, Senior Managing Director, General Counsel, is an experienced and well-respected member of the legal and compliance community. Mr. Amoruso oversees all legal, compliance, and regulatory matters at Knight, and is an integral part of developing the market structure views of the firm. In October 1999, Mr. Amoruso joined the company as Chief Compliance Officer and Assistant General Counsel of Knight Securities, L.P., a subsidiary later renamed Knight Equity Markets, L.P. He was named Chief Compliance Officer of the parent company in June 2003 and General Counsel in May 2007. Before joining Knight, Mr. Amoruso spent a decade with FINRA's District No. 10 office in New York, most recently as Deputy Director. He also was Chief Counsel with FINRA, overseeing and prosecuting hundreds of disciplinary actions. Mr. Amoruso has a BBA in banking, finance and investments from Hofstra University and a J.D. from Hofstra University School of Law. He serves on numerous industry committees and is a frequent speaker at industry conferences.

James J. Angel is Associate Professor of Finance at the McDonough School of Business at Georgetown University. Professor Angel is a financial expert whose research focuses on the operation of financial markets in the United States and other countries. For the year 1999–2000 Professor Angel was the Visiting Academic Fellow at the NASD, where he participated in several studies of The Nasdaq Stock Market, Inc. He currently serves on the OTCBB Advisory Board, and he has served as Chair of the Nasdaq Economic Advisory Board. After graduating from the California Institute of Technology, he began his career as a Rate Engineer at Pacific Gas and Electric Company. Following an MBA from Harvard Business School, he worked developing equity risk models at BARRA, Inc. "Dr. Jim" earned a PhD in finance from the University of California at Berkeley, and then joined the faculty of Georgetown in 1991. Professor Angel has published in numerous prestigious academic journals, including the Journal of Finance and the Journal of Financial Economics. He has appeared on many radio and television programs, and is quoted regularly in major newspapers. Professor Angel has also served as a consultant to broker-dealers, stock markets, and law firms.

Doug Atkin is the founder and managing partner of Financial Technology Investors. Prior to Majestic, Doug was President and CEO of Instinet Group, where he conducted Instinet's IPO (NASDAQ: INGP). He also developed Instinet's research, as well as its international trading and correspondent clearing businesses, and led a consortium of nine global brokerage firms that took a majority stake in the virt-x stock exchange. Doug serves as a member of the Board of Directors of Starmine, WR Hambrecht, and Tamale Software. He has been named twice to the Online Finance 30, Institutional Investor's annual ranking of the most important leaders in international e-finance. Doug is a graduate of Tufts University.

Leslie Boni is head of Quantitative Strategies and Performance Analytics at UNX. Prior to working at UNX, Leslie served as a visiting academic scholar at the US Securities and Exchange Commission, a finance professor at the University of New Mexico, and as a lecturer at the University of Southern California. Her research has been published in the Journal of Financial and Quantitative Analysis; the Journal of Financial Markets; the Journal of Money, Credit, and Banking; the Financial Analysts Journal; and she has authored several Brookings Institute Papers on Financial Services. Prior to earning a PhD in finance from the University of Colorado at Boulder, she worked for 15 years in the oil industry as chemical engineer, trader, risk manager, and consultant. Leslie also holds a BS in chemical engineering from Northwestern University.

Kevin Callahan is Head of Sales and Strategy at JonesTrading Institutional Services LLC. Prior to joining JonesTrading, Mr. Callahan was a management consultant at McKinsey & Company, where he worked in the Operations Effectiveness practice. Later, Mr. Callahan was Vice President and General Manager of the Software division of Opus360 Corporation and Vice President and General Manager of the Property & Casualty business at MagnaCare LLC. Mr. Callahan is a frequent writer and speaker on topics related to business management and profitability. Mr. Callahan graduated from Yale University with a BA in History. He was a two-time All-Ivy-League running back and a member of the 1990 GTE Academic All-American Team. He holds a Master's in International Affairs from Columbia University and an MBA from the MIT Sloan School of Management.

Paul Davis retired from TIAA-CREF in February of 2006. He served as a senior managing director, as head of trading and as co-head of quantitative portfolio management. He continues at TIAA-CREF in a part time capacity working on special projects. He has an undergraduate degree from West Virginia University and a doctorate in mathematics from Carnegie Mellon University. Before beginning his Wall Street career, he taught mathematics at the university level. Along with more customary retirement pursuits, he is writing papers with Professors Robert Schwartz and Mike Pagano as well as planning a new business enterprise that introduces a new (and better) way to evaluate the investment process.

Ian Domowitz is a Managing Director at Investment Technology Group, Inc., responsible for ITG Solutions Network, Inc., and a member of the company's Management and Executive Committees. Prior to joining the company in 2001, he served as the Mary Jean and Frank P. Smeal Professor of Finance at Pennsylvania State University and previously was the Household International Research Professor of Economics at Northwestern University. A former member of the NASD's Bond Market Transparency Committee, he also served as chair of the Economic Advisory Board of the NASD. Mr. Domowitz has held positions with Northwestern's Kellogg Graduate School of Management, Columbia University, the Commodity Futures Trading Commission, the International Monetary Fund and the World Bank. He is currently a Fellow of the Program in the Law and Economics of Capital Markets at Columbia University.

Alfred Eskandar is Global Head of Corporate Strategy and a founding employee of Liquidnet Holdings, Inc. Liquidnet is the world's institutional marketplace that facilitates institutional equities trading for more than 550 asset management firms worldwide, with trading in 29 markets across the globe. Alfred is responsible for Liquidnet's strategic initiatives, alliances and investments. In March 2007, Alfred led the acquisition of Miletus Trading, LLC, a leading quantitative and program trading broker–dealer, and he served as President and Chief Executive Officer during its integration. Prior to that, he helped shape the brand identity of Liquidnet by serving as its head of marketing from 2000 to 2004. From 1996 to 2000, Alfred headed business development for the operations, trading and technology division of Thomson Financial's Investment Marketing Group. Prior to that, Alfred helped launch Securities Industries News, which was acquired by Thomson Financial Services in 1996. Alfred holds a BBA in Finance & Economics from Baruch College.

Fred Federspiel is the President and founder of Pipeline Trading Systems, a rapidly growing independent and anonymous large block trading venue. Fred earned a PhD in Experimental Nuclear and Particle Physics from the University of Illinois at Champaign/Urbana, and then worked at Los Alamos National Laboratory as a nuclear physicist. Fred became very interested in understanding how market structure impacts the ability to efficiently trade large orders while working at the Bios Group, a complexity science consulting firm founded by Ernst & Young. This interest culminated in the founding of Pipeline in 1999, and ultimately in the launch of the Pipeline block trading platform on September 9, 2004.

Robert Gauvain has more than 30 years of industry experience, including 22 years with Pioneer Investments. He currently directs equity trading operations for Pioneer Investments, USA, including domestic and international markets. Mr. Gauvain's first position at Pioneer Investments in 1984 was equity trader covering NASDAQ and small cap issues. He began his career as a floor trader at Hawthorne Securities, and also traded NASDAQ and unlisted securities at Moors & Cabot. He is a member of both the Boston and National Security Traders Associations and holds a BS degree from Suffolk University.

Joe Gawronski is the President/COO of Rosenblatt Securities. Joe is formerly a securities lawyer with Sullivan & Cromwell, a Vice President in the equities division with Salomon Smith Barney and COO of Linx LLC, an alternative block trading system. He received his BA in Public and International Affairs at Princeton's Woodrow Wilson School and his JD from Harvard Law School. He is an Allied

Member of the NYSE, a member of the NYSE Hearing Board, a member of the Advisory Boards of both the *Journal of Trading* and *Wall Street & Technology* magazine, a term member of the Council on Foreign Relations, the author or co-author of several published papers on equity market structure and a frequent lecturer, moderator and panelist on the topic.

Daniel Gray is currently the Senior Special Counsel for Market Structure in the Division of Market Regulation, US Securities and Exchange Commission. Since 1999, he has worked on a variety of SEC market structure initiatives, including Regulation NMS (2005), disclosure of order execution quality and order routing practices (2001), the Market Fragmentation Concept Release (2000), and the Market Information Concept Release (1999). His responsibilities for Regulation NMS relate primarily to the Order Protection Rule, Access Rule, and Market Data Rules and Plan Amendments. He previously worked as an Assistant General Counsel of Ernst & Young, as counsel to SEC Commissioner Philip R. Lochner, Jr., and as an attorney in the Office of Chief Counsel of the Division of Market Regulation. Mr. Gray is a 1983 graduate of the Duke University School of Law.

William Harts is a management consultant known in the financial services industry as a pioneer of algorithmic trading as well as an authority on financial market structure and applied technology. Mr. Harts has most recently been Managing Director and Head of Equity Strategy for Banc of America Securities. This position included responsibility for development of the firm's electronic and algorithmic trading businesses, including its industry-leading Electronic Algorithmic Strategy Execution (EASE) and InstaQuote direct market access products as well as the Quantitative Strategies research group. He was Chairman of the Bank's NYSE Specialist business, guiding it through an especially tumultuous reinvention process. Mr. Harts also had broad responsibility for the Equity Division's strategic planning, investments and joint ventures. In that capacity he led investments in the Chicago Stock Exchange and the BIDS Alternative Trading System and managed the integration of two other acquisitions into the bank. Prior to joining the bank, Mr. Harts held the position of Executive Vice President for Corporate Strategy for The NASDAQ Stock Market, Inc. where his responsibilities included the planning and development of strategic initiatives. He was also a consultant to the NASD, assisting with the design and implementation of the industrywide Alternative Display Facility, and National Financial Services (a division of Fidelity Management & Research) advising on restructuring their brokerage business. Before moving to NASDAQ, Mr. Harts was Managing Director of Strategic Business Development for the Global Equity Division of Salomon Smith Barney with responsibility for the firm's partnerships, joint ventures and investments as well as market structure developments relating to equity trading. Before taking on that role, Mr. Harts was head of the firm's Global Program Trading Department for 7 years, with responsibility for desks in New York, London and Tokyo. He began at SSB in September 1993 after working at Lehman Brothers where he established a pioneering automated market making and trading operation for the Worldwide Equities Division. Prior to that, he worked at Goldman, Sachs & Co. for 4 years with Fischer Black in their Quantitative Strategies Group developing equity derivative trading systems. Mr. Harts is a featured speaker and panelist on electronic trading and market structure issues at many industry forums. He has spoken at the SIFMA 2007 Annual Conference, the FPL Americas Electronic Trading Conference, the Securities Industry Association Market Structure Conference, the Pace University Center for the Study of Equity Markets' Securities Industry Conference, and the Baruch College Zicklin School of Business' Regulation of US Equity Markets Conference. He is quoted extensively in the books, "Regulation of U.S. Equity Markets" and "Call Auction Trading: New Answers to Old Questions." He was a member of the SEC's Special Advisory Committee on Market Information and the Nasdaq UTP Advisory Committee. Mr. Harts served as a Director and Vice Chairman and member of the Board of the Philadelphia Stock Exchange from 1994 through 1999. He has been a member of the Board of Directors of JapanCross, an electronic trading system for Japanese equities that he helped establish. He has served on the boards of BRUT and MarketXT, two electronic communications networks, as well as the managing advisory committee for Primex Trading, an alternative trading system. Before coming to Wall Street, Mr. Harts worked in the information technology industry for more than 12 years and is the developer of a best selling data communications software package. His articles on various aspects of the computer industry have been published internationally in PC Magazine.

Frank Hatheway is Chief Economist of the Nasdaq Stock Market, Inc., and is responsible for a variety of projects and initiatives to support the Nasdaq market and improve its market structure. Prior to joining Nasdaq, Dr. Hatheway was a finance professor at Penn State University and a researcher in market microstructure. He has authored academic articles in the *Journal of Finance, Journal of Financial Intermediation* and other leading finance journals. Dr. Hatheway has served as an Economic Fellow and Senior Research Scholar with the US Security and Exchange Commission. Dr. Hatheway received his PhD in Economics from Princeton University.

Richard Holowczak is presently an Associate Professor of Computer Information Systems and is Director of the Bert W. and Sandra Wasserman Trading Floor/ Subotnick Financial Services Center in the Zicklin School of Business, Baruch College, City University of New York. Dr. Holowczak also directs the Options Data Warehouse project at the Subotnick Center. He holds a BS in Computer Science from the College of New Jersey, an MS in Computer Science from the New Jersey Institute of Technology, and MBA and PhD degrees from Rutgers University. His research focuses on financial information systems, digital libraries, electronic commerce and networked information systems. He has published articles in IEEE Computer Journal, IEEE Transactions on Knowledge and Data Engineering, Communications of the ACM, Online Information Review, ACM Computing Surveys, Journal of Education for Business, Journal of the Academy of Business Education, the Journal of Financial Education and Review of Derivatives Research. His research has been supported by the Professional Staff Congress-CUNY, NASA and the National Science Foundation. He is a member of the IEEE Computer

Society, the Association for Computing Machinery (ACM) and the Academy of Business Education.

Richard Ketchum has been chief executive officer of NYSE Regulation, Inc., since 2006. He is a member of the NYSE Regulation board of directors. Mr. Ketchum is also non-executive chairman of the board of the Financial Industry Regulatory Authority (FINRA). He also serves as chairman of the regulatory committee of the World Federation of Exchanges. Mr. Ketchum had served as the first chief regulatory officer of the New York Stock Exchange since March 8, 2004. From June 2003 to March 2004, Mr. Ketchum was General Counsel of the Corporate and Investment Bank of Citigroup, Inc., and a member of the unit's planning group, Business Practices Committee and Risk Management Committee. Previously, he spent 12 years at NASD and the NASDAQ Stock Market, Inc., where he served as president of both organizations. Prior to working at NASD and Nasdaq, Mr. Ketchum was at the US Securities and Exchange Commission for 14 years, eight of those as director of the division of Market Regulation. Mr. Ketchum earned his JD from the New York University School of Law in 1975 and his BA from Tufts University in 1972. He is a member of the bar in both New York and the District of Columbia.

David Krell is a founder of ISE and was President & CEO until December 31, 2007. From 1997 to 1998, he was Chairman and co-founder of K-Squared Research, LLC, a financial services consulting firm. From 1984 to 1997, Mr. Krell was Vice President, Options and Index Products, of the New York Stock Exchange where he managed marketing, systems and new product introductions for the division. From 1981 to 1984, Mr. Krell was First Vice President at the Chicago Board Options Exchange, responsible for the management and operation of the Marketing and Sales Division. Mr. Krell was also a Vice President of Merrill Lynch from 1978 to 1981 and founded its Managed Options Service. Mr. Krell is active in numerous industry groups. He was a Director on the Board of the International Federation of Technical Analysts, a president of the Market Technicians Association and a Director on the Board of The Options Clearing Corporation. Mr. Krell formerly was an Adjunct Professor at Rutgers University Graduate School of Management and at the Graduate School of Baruch College. He has taught, coordinated and directed numerous seminars and workshops at the New York Institute of Finance.

James Leman is Head of Capital Markets and is a Principal at Westwater. Jim is currently consulting after having spent years leading global electronic trading and external connectivity, global operations management and regulatory groups at Citigroup, HSBC and the New York Stock Exchange and their affiliates. Jim also served as the President of SunGard BRASS. Jim has in-depth skills in financial and operational aspects of the brokerage industry, and continues to lead firms and the industry, in creation of innovative technologies and standards for trading and managing the processing of securities transactions. Recognized as one of the top technology innovators of the 1990s by Wall Street & Technology Magazine, Jim is a founding member of the FIX (Financial Information Exchange) Industry committee; he led the global creation of the FIX committee in Europe, Japan, and

Asia. Jim was also a founding member of Thompson/DTCC Omgeo (US) Advisory committee. Jim holds a BS in Accounting St. Peter's College and an MBA in finance from Fordham University.

Robert McCooey is Senior Vice President of the Capital Markets Group and is responsible for managing NASDAQ's efforts to engage private equity firms, investment banks and institutional investors on key NASDAQ issues, initiatives and services. Mr. McCooey joined The NASDAQ Stock Market, Inc. (NASDAQ) in December 2006. The Capital Markets Group is the first centralized group at NASDAQ that examines customer needs across all NASDAQ business units. In his new role, Mr. McCooey will work to further NASDAQ's mission among private equity, investment banks and institutional investors, aiming to enhance their experience with NASDAQ and supporting their business goals and growth plans. Prior to joining NASDAQ, Mr. McCooey served as the Chief Executive Officer of The Griswold Company, an agency he founded in 1988 which served prominent and developing buy-side institutions.

Oscar Onyema is Senior Vice President and Chief Administrative Officer of the American Stock Exchange. Mr. Onyema serves as a primary liaison among various Amex operating divisions, the trading floor community, and external constituents. In addition, he is responsible for strategy and competitive analysis, Membership and Registration Department and Market Data Services Department. Mr. Onyema has been instrumental in Amex's preparation for Regulation NMS, and serves on several industry committees including CTA Operating Committee, NASDAQ UTP Plan Operating Committee, and SIFMA/FIF Regulation NMS working group. Mr. Onyema joined the Amex in January 2001, and has served in various positions, most recently as Vice President and Chief Administrative Officer. Before joining the Amex, Mr. Onyema worked at the New York Mercantile Exchange (NYMEX) as Senior Analyst, Business Planning and Development. He also worked at DPMS (IBM Business Partner) as a Marketing Executive marketing IBM mid-range systems. Mr. Onyema received an MBA in Finance and Investments from Baruch College in New York City. He served as an adjunct lecturer at the Economics Department of Pace University for 5 years, and is a frequent public speaker on market structure and market data issues.

Michael S. Pagano is an Associate Professor of Finance at Villanova University. Professor Pagano has conducted several empirical analyses related to various issues in market microstructure, financial institution management, risk management, cost of capital estimation, and interest rate determination. He has published in numerous finance journals such as the *Journal of Financial Economics, Journal of Banking and Finance, Journal of International Money and Finance, Journal of Portfolio Management*, and the *Financial Analysts Journal*. In addition to serving on the editorial boards of two academic journals, Professor Pagano has been a Fulbright Scholar at the University of Costa Rica and has received awards for both teaching excellence and academic scholarship. Prior to earning his doctorate and joining the Villanova University faculty, Professor Pagano spent over 10 years in the financial services industry. He holds the Chartered Financial Analyst (CFA®) designation and has experience both in commercial lending activities at Citibank and in investment valuation analysis at a financial consulting firm, International Capital Markets Corp., as well as Reuters PLC. In addition to his duties at Villanova University, Professor Pagano has been a consultant to several companies including Citibank, PaineWebber, Fidelity Investments, GTE Investments, Philadelphia Suburban Corp., Aqua America, and Bank Julius Baer. Professor Pagano is a commentator on current market structure issues and has been frequently quoted in various media sources such as the *Wall Street Journal*, *New York Times*, *Financial Times*, *CNBC*, *Bloomberg TV*, and *Bloomberg Radio*.

Bob Pisani has been a CNBC correspondent since 1990. He has covered real estate and corporate management, and now reports on Wall Street from the floor of the New York Stock Exchange. He was nominated twice for a CableACE Award, in 1993 and 1995. Prior to joining CNBC, Pisani co-authored "Investing in Land: How to be a Successful Developer." He also taught real estate development at the Wharton School of Business at The University of Pennsylvania for 5 years with his father. Pisani learned the real estate business from his father, Ralph Pisani, a retired real estate developer. Since April 2006, Andreas Preuß is a member of the Executive Board of Deutsche Boerse AG and the Chief Executive Officer of Eurex Zurich AG, Eurex Frankfurt AG and Eurex Clearing AG. Since June 2006, he is also a member of the Management Board of Eurex Deutschland as well as Chairman of the Management Board of the Frankfurt Stock Exchange. From 2002 to 2006, he was the Chief Operating Officer and a member of the Board of Mako Group, London, a leading trading house and market maker in exchange traded fixed income and index options. From 2000 to 2001, Preuß was President of Trading Technologies in Evanston, Chicago. From 1990 to 2000, he held leading positions within Deutsche Boerse AG, lastly being a member of the Eurex Management Board, responsible for Business Development, Marketing and Sales. Preuß made a significant contribution in the setup of the Deutsche Terminboerse (DTB), the predecessor of Eurex. He was also directly involved in the founding and setting up of Eurex to the largest derivatives exchange worldwide. Preuß started his career at Dresdner Bank AG in Cologne. Afterwards he was employed as a Senior Consultant at Andersen Consulting in Frankfurt. He studied Economics at the University of Hamburg, majoring in International Management, Finance and Commercial law.

James Ross is vice president of NYSE MatchPoint and oversees the development and operations of the equity crossing facility for NYSE Euronext. Prior to joining NYSE in July of 2006, Mr. Ross was CEO of MatchPoint Trading, a firm dedicated to the business of electronic call market trading. From 1989 to 2003, he spearheaded Instinet's Global Crossing business. During that period, Mr. Ross built daily US crossing volume to 17 million shares a day, established Instinet's international crossing business, launched JapanCross – the first Japanese equity crossing service (with Nikko Salomon Smith Barney), as well as multi-currency, UK, VWAP and FX crosses.

Robert A. Schwartz is Marvin M. Speiser Professor of Finance and University Distinguished Professor in the Zicklin School of Business, Baruch College, CUNY. Before joining the Baruch faculty in 1997, he was Professor of Finance and Economics and Yamaichi Faculty Fellow at New York University's Leonard N. Stern School of Business, where he had been a member of the faculty since 1965. Professor Schwartz received his PhD in Economics from Columbia University. His research is in the area of financial economics, with a primary focus on the structure of securities markets. He has published 60 refereed journal articles, 5 authored books, and 12 edited books, including *The Equity Trader Course* (co-authored with Reto Francioni and Bruce Weber) Wiley & Sons, 2006, *Equity Markets in Action: The Fundamentals of Liquidity, Market Structure and Trading* (co-authored with Reto Francioni) Wiley & Sons, 2004, and *Reshaping the Equity Markets: A Guide for the 1990s*, Harper Business, 1991 (reissued by Business One Irwin, 1993). He has served as a consultant to various market centers including the New York Stock Exchange, the American Stock Exchange, Nasdaq, the London Stock Exchange, Instinet, the Arizona Stock Exchange, Deutsche Börse, and the Bolsa Mexicana. From April 1983 to April 1988, he was an associate editor of *The Journal of Finance*, and he is currently an associate editor of the *Review of Quantitative Finance and Accounting,* the *Review of Pacific Basin Financial Markets and Policies*, and *The Journal of Entrepreneurial Finance & Business Ventures*, and is a member of the advisory boards of *International Finance* and *The Journal of Trading*. In December 1995, Professor Schwartz was named the first chairman of Nasdaq's Economic Advisory Board, and he served on the EAB until Spring 1999. He is developer, with Bruce Weber, of the trading and market structure simulation, TraderEx (http://www.etraderex.com/).

Daniel Shaffer is the head trader/owner of Shaffer Asset Management. Mr. Shaffer began his career in 1983 as a floor trader on the New York Futures Exchange (NYFE). Through the 1980s, he was with Bear Stearns, Coopers & Lybrand, and Hambrecht & Quist. In 1991, Mr. Shaffer began the development of computerized trading systems based on price and time parameters to quantify psychology of the markets. In 1999, he began trading individual managed commodity accounts under his firm, Shaffer Asset Management, which is registered as a CTA and CPO with the NFA and CTFC. In 2003, Mr. Shaffer introduced the Shaffer Foreign Exchange trading program utilizing the same computerized trading systems that he applies to the commodity futures markets. Shaffer Asset Management is also the General Partner and Trading Advisor to the Shaffer Partners, LP Fund which is comprised of both the Commodity-II and Foreign Exchange Programs. Mr. Shaffer is a frequent guest speaker on the subject of non-emotional and systematic trading.

Douglas Shulman became the 47th Commissioner of Internal Revenue and began his 5-year term on March 24, 2008. He presides over the nation's tax administration system, which collects approximately $2.4 trillion in tax revenue that funds most government operations and public services. He manages an agency of over 100,000 employees and a budget of approximately $11 billion. As Commissioner, Shulman has emphasized a balanced program between taxpayer service and tax enforcement. The IRS goals are improving service to make voluntary compliance easier for taxpayers while at the same time enforcing the law to make sure everyone meets their obligation to pay taxes. Commissioner Shulman has stressed several key initiatives during his tenure. In the face of increasing globalization of tax administration, he has stepped up IRS activity on a variety of international and corporate tax issues. During the financial downturn, the IRS balanced demands of the economic stimulus program with regular tax administration work to ensure that 106 million refund checks and 116 million stimulus payments reached the hands of taxpayers in 2008. In the face of an aging workforce, Commissioner Shulman created the Workforce of Tomorrow task force to ensure that in 5 years the IRS has the leadership and workforce ready for the next 15 years and to help make the IRS the best place to work in government. Commissioner Shulman came to the IRS from the Financial Industry Regulatory Authority (FINRA), the private-sector regulator of all securities firms doing business in the United States. As vice chairman, he was responsible for strategy, services and operations. He served in the same role at the National Association of Securities Dealers (NASD) before its 2007 consolidation with New York Stock Exchange Member Regulation, which resulted in the formation of FINRA. After joining NASD in 2000, Commissioner Shulman played an integral role in restructuring the company, led the negotiations of the sale of the NASDAQ stock market and American Stock Exchange, oversaw the launch of industry-wide bond market transparency and modernized NASD's technology operations. Earlier in his career, Commissioner Shulman was involved with several start-up organizations, was a vice president of a private investment firm and served as Senior Policy Advisor and then Chief of Staff of the National Commission on Restructuring the IRS. Commissioner Shulman holds a BA from Williams College, an MPA from Harvard University's John F. Kennedy School of Government and a JD from Georgetown University Law Center.

Erik Sirri is the Director of Market Regulation at the US Securities and Exchange Commission. In this role he is responsible to the Commission for the administration of all matters relating to the regulation of stock and option exchanges, national securities associations, brokers, dealers, and clearing agencies. He is on leave from Babson College where he is a Professor of Finance. His research interests include the interaction of securities law and finance, securities market structure, securities trading, and the investment management industry. From 1996 to 1999, Sirri served as the Chief Economist of the Securities and Exchange Commission. Before joining the SEC, Sirri was an Assistant Professor of Finance at the Harvard Business School from 1989 to 1995. Sirri received his BS in Astronomy from the California Institute of Technology in 1979, an MBA from the University of California, Irvine, in 1984, and his PhD in Finance from the University of California, Los Angeles, in 1990. Before becoming a professor, he worked on planetary astronomy missions for NASA and on space surveillance sensors in the aerospace industry. His published writings appear in academic journals, practitioner journals, and books. He has served as a Governor of the Boston Stock Exchange and a member of the regulatory board of the Boston Options Exchange (BOX). He has consulted for securities firms, stock exchanges, mutual fund companies, issuers, and information vendors on a variety of regulatory and business matters.

Nic Stuchfield has spent his whole career in the Financial Services industry and has a unique range of experience. During 16 years with Barclays (and its former Investment Banking subsidiary BZW), Nic progressively increased his responsibilities, becoming COO of the global Equities business of BZW until 1995. He then played a major role in the acquisition of Wells Fargo Nikko Investment Advisers by Barclays, relocating to the San Francisco HQ of the newly-formed Barclays Global Investors, the world's largest index fund manager. There he was both COO and Global Head of Indexed Investments. He returned to the UK in 1997 to become the CEO of the Tradepoint Stock Exchange (now called Virt-x), where he was responsible for restoring relationships between the exchange and the investment banking community. Nic left Tradepoint in the middle of 1999 and created the Stuchfield Consultancy in the autumn of that year, where he was Managing Director until June 2004. In 2001, Nic became a non-executive Director (and subsequently Chairman) of Totem Market Valuations Limited, the world leader in derivatives valuations, culminating in the sale of TMV to Mark-It Partners in mid-2004. In mid-2003, Nic was invited to become Managing Director of EDX London, the derivatives exchange subsidiary of the London Stock Exchange and OMX of Sweden and, in early 2004, his role at the LSE was expanded to include becoming Head of Corporate Development, a function which includes corporate strategy, research and business planning.

Larry Tabb is the founder and CEO of TABB Group, the financial markets' research and strategic advisory firm focused exclusively on capital markets. Founded in 2003 and based on the interview-based research methodology of "first-person knowledge" he developed, TABB Group analyzes and quantifies the investing value chain from the fiduciary, investment manager, broker, exchange and custodian, helping senior business leaders gain a truer understanding of financial markets issues. Larry has published industry research analyzing ECNs; fixed income, equity and foreign exchange trading systems; back-office trade processing systems; broker workstations; analytical trading tools; infrastructure development tools; and foreign and emerging market technologies. He has written extensively on the changing market structure, exchanges and regulatory issues and business continuity as well as new technology trends in cost management, risk management, order management, best execution, algorithmic trading, dark pools, multi- and cross-asset trading, liquidity management, FIX, STP, connectivity, custody and advances in emerging technologies. Before founding TABB Group, he was vice president of TowerGroup's Securities & Investments practice where he managed research across the capital markets, investment management, retail brokerage and wealth management segments. As the founding member of TowerGroup's securities and investments business, he was instrumental in growing the business into a global brand representing over 150 research clients around the world. Quoted extensively and in virtually all industry and general news publications, he has been cited in The Wall Street Journal, Financial Times, Associated Press, The New York Times, CNN, Bloomberg, CNBC, Reuters, Dow Jones News, Barron's, Forbes, Business Week, Financial News, Wall Street & Technology, Securities Industry News, Waters, Global Investment Technology, Computerworld, eWEEK, American Banker,

The Banker, Lipper HedgeWorld, Hedge Fund Review and Wall Street Letter. He continues to be a featured speaker at major industry and business conferences throughout the US, Europe, Asia and Canada. He currently writes monthly columns discussing business and technology issues germane to the global securities industry as a contributing editor for Wall Street & Technology and Advanced Trading magazines. From 1997 to 2001, he was the author of benchmark industry technology surveys co-sponsored by TowerGroup and the Securities Industry Association (published biennially): Technology Trends in the Securities Industry: Investing in Tomorrow's Infrastructure, 2001 and Technology Trends in the Securities Industry: Transition to an Online World, 1999; and co-authored the 1997 Technology Trends in the Securities Industry: Spending, Strategies, Challenges & Change – all in-depth analyses of technology trends and spending within the securities industry that were widely distributed and quoted. Prior to joining TowerGroup, he managed business analysis for Lehman Brothers' Trading Services Division and was responsible for overseeing the specification, testing and implementation of dozens of major systems during his tenure. He was also in charge of capital markets technology planning at Lehman Brothers where he developed 1- and 3-year technology plans from 1988 through 1992. He began his career managing various operations for the North American Investment Bank of Citibank, where he managed front office trading and finance operations, various back-office money market operations and, for US Treasury debt, proprietary trading clearance and settlement operations.

John Thain was chief executive officer of the NYSE Group at the time of the conference, and before that he served as chief executive officer of the New York Stock Exchange from 2004 through 2005. Prior to joining the NYSE, Mr. Thain served as president and chief operating officer of Goldman Sachs Group, Inc. since July 2003 and was previously president and co-chief operating officer from May 1999 through June 2003; he had been a director since 1998, prior to joining the NYSE. He was president and co-chief operating officer of The Goldman Sachs Group, L.P. in 1999. From 1994 to 1999, he served as chief financial officer and head of operations, technology and finance. From 1995 to 1997, he was also co-chief executive officer for European operations. He is a member of The MIT Corporation, the Dean's Advisory Council – MIT/Sloan School of Management, INSEAD – US National Advisory Board, the James Madison Council of the Library of Congress and the Federal Reserve Bank of New York's International Capital Markets Advisory Committee. He is also a member of the French-American Foundation, as well as a governor of the New York-Presbyterian Foundation, Inc., a trustee of New York-Presbyterian Hospital and a General Trustee of Howard University. Mr. Thain received an MBA from Harvard University in 1979 and a BS degree from Massachusetts Institute of Technology in 1977.

Joseph Wald is CEO of EdgeTrade, Inc. In 1996, Joe set out with Kyle Zasky to establish an agency-only broker that would re-define how traders gain open access to emerging electronic trading tools and anonymous, uncompromised execution services; this mission remains at the core of EdgeTrade's business. Joe was in college when his interest in Wall Street took hold, starting with a position at Datek Securities. Joe's experiences at Datek began in the back-office and within 2 years he was working as a broker and market maker. Not soon after, Joe formed EdgeTrade: "Traders who are clients of EdgeTrade understand that we get it, and the 'it' is a platform and execution environment working together to give them complete and practical functionality, coupled with a level playing field in terms of accessing liquidity, best execution and price transparency. EdgeTrade's independent, agency-only model is in stark contrast with bulge-bracket firms and their numerous internal, competing interests that prevent traders from having the tools and services they need and want. EdgeTrade is fueling a paradigm shift that centers on changing the perception of institutional traders who want what we are willing to offer them."

Robert Wood is a Distinguished Professor of Finance at the University of Memphis. Professor Wood previously taught at Penn State University for 14 years and NYU for 1 year. His education includes a PhD in Finance from the University of Pittsburgh, a Masters in Operations Research from Stanford University, and a Bachelors in Economics from the University of Washington. He was a member of the Presidential Task Force on Market Mechanisms (The Brady Commission) that studied the market crash in 1987, and a founding member of the NASD Economic Advisory Board. Professor Wood is the founder and Executive Director of the Institute for the Study of Security Markets, a nonprofit Educational Foundation that promotes securities markets research by providing transactions data to academic institutions. He has consulted for various stock exchanges and investment firms around the world. Professor Wood servers on the editorial boards of the Journal of Banking and Finance and the Journal of Trading.

Index

Breinigsville, PA USA
12 March 2010
233999BV00012B/103/P